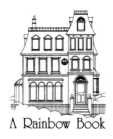

A Rainbow Book

Praise for Making Real Love Happen—

"*Making Real Love Happen* is the most profound and effective relationship book on the market today. It provides tools that produce life-changing results. Every reader will find a mirror of their relationships and a reliable model for creating the intimacy their heart desires."

—Harville Hendrix, Ph.D., author of bestseller
Getting the Love You Want

"The tightest, most succinct book I've ever read. Every other sentence is profound—it's truth after truth after truth."

—Julie Ziglar Norman, Zig Ziglar's personal editor

"Joyce Buckner is one of the finest minds in the field of human relations today. She artfully takes the very complex interactions in relationships and reveals them to the reader with ease and compassion."

—Pat Love, Ed.D., author of
The Truth About Love

"Who should read this book? Intelligent, responsible adults who are interested in growing their own inner 'child' wherever s/he shows up and in ending the repressive forces that pass down from generation to generation. A splendid book!"

—Mark W. Shulkin, M.D.,
Fellow of the American Psychiatric Society; faculty member,
Medical College of Pennsylvania/Hahnemann University

"Joyce Buckner lives what she teaches. She embodies the empathy, respect, and authenticity that are the heart of the Real Love she writes about in this wonderfully wise and potent book about relationships. Her work inspires, empowers, and heals! Reading this book and practicing what you learn will enhance all the important relationships in your life."

—Martha Baldwin Beveridge, M.S.S.W.,
author of *Loving Your Partner without Losing Your Self*

"This is an important book. Dr. Buckner's processes create connection between partners. By learning and putting her ideas into practice, you can create life-long love."

—Jon Carlson, Psy.D., Ed.D,
Distinguished Professor, Governors State University,
author of *Time for A Better Marriage*

"Dr. Buckner has distilled the complex concepts of relationship theory into a brilliant model and an understandable and beautiful book. Easy to read, a great joy to share, full of wisdom."

—Marjorie Barlow, Ph.D., author of
The Possible Woman

Making Real Love Happen

The New ERA of Intimacy

JOYCE BUCKNER, PH.D.

Rainbow Books, Inc.
FLORIDA

Library of Congress Cataloging-in-Publication Data

Buckner, Joyce P., 1937-
  Making real love happen : the new era of intimacy / Joyce P. Buckner.— 1st ed.
    p. cm.
  Includes bibliographical references and index.
  ISBN 1-56825-094-0 (hardcover : alk. paper)
  1. Man-woman relationships. 2. Intimacy (Psychology) I. Title.
  HQ801.B874 2004
  306.7—dc22

                              2003028315

Making Real Love Happen: The New ERA of Intimacy
© 2004 Joyce Buckner, Ph.D.
ISBN 1-56825-094-0

Visit Dr. Buckner's websites at
www.JoyceBuckner.com and www.MakingRealLoveHappen.com

Permissions can be found in the acknowledgments pages.

Publisher/Editorial Offices
        Rainbow Books, Inc.
        P. O. Box 430
        Highland City, Florida
        33846-0430
        Telephone: (863) 648-4420
        Facsimile: (863) 647-5951
        Email: RBIbooks@aol.com

Order Information
        Booksellers/Retailers: Ingram, B&T, Book Clearing House
        Individuals telephone 1-800-431-1579
        Individuals online: www.AllBookStores.com

To

My Mom—who's loved me longest,

My Dad—who loved me until he died,

My adult children—Cheryl, Bucky, and Chris—who've taught me much about loving,

My husband, Sandy—who shares the crucible of loving with me every day,

And my grandchildren—John, Christina, Natalie, Jake, and Austin—who I hope will inherit and create an increasingly loving world.

Contents

PART I
UNDERSTANDING RELATIONSHIP DYNAMICS

Foreword

Myths take a long time to die, even when the evidence against them is monumental. A prime example is "After the wedding, they lived happily ever after." Long dramatized in fairy tales and ancient lore is the belief that the only thing marriages need to last forever is romantic love.

In *Making Real Love Happen—The New ERA of Intimacy*, Dr. Buckner compassionately dismantles the myth and makes it clear that the absence of romantic love is not the problem in troubled marriages. Rather, she identifies the true culprit as each partner's inability to break away from ingrained behaviors driven by a lifetime of deep unmet needs. By showing the reader— through real-life examples—how s/he undermines their relationships and what to do differently, the reader's potential and power to make real love happen is awakened.

In an extraordinary mix of poetic and scientific language, Dr. Buckner describes the actual nature of lasting love. The communication process that debuts herein has the proven power to heal troubled relationships and provide a solid foundation for mature love.

Because this book is loaded with practical insight and tools that produce life-changing results, *Making Real Love Happen—The New ERA of Intimacy* is the most profound and effective relationship book on the market today.

Harville Hendrix, Ph.D.
New Jersey

Acknowledgments

To the many whose contributions made this book possible, I am grateful. To name a few:

Those with whom I've had personal relationships.

The hundreds of couples and individual clients who over the past thirty years have disclosed, described, and demonstrated relationship dynamics.

Harville Hendrix, with whom I've studied and collaborated for over 20 years in the development of Imago Relationship Therapy, and Charles Truax, who was my mentor in Interpersonal Skills training. These two teachers were particularly influential in sparking me to create the model *The New ERA* (Empathy, Respect and Authenticity) *of Intimacy*, which debuts in *Making Real Love Happen*. Other teachers and authors who have been particularly influential include Merl Bonney, Martin Buber, John Enright, Milton H. Erickson, Moshe Feldenkrais, Jean Houston, Ken Keyes Jr., Alfred Korzybski, Margaret Mahler, Paul McLean, Wilder Penfield, John Pierrakos, Daniel Siegel, Richard Stuart and Danah Zohar.

All of the aforementioned stand on the shoulders of masters who have gone before. I thank these unmentioned pioneers in the study of human behavior as well.

Appreciation goes to those who critiqued the manuscript in various stages of development, including personal friends and family, and especially my husband, Sanford Reitman, M.D., who believed in me and supported this undertaking from the beginning.

I also want to give a special thanks to 1) my agent, Susan Crawford of the Crawford Literary Agency, whose encouragement and undying optimism kept me from giving up on the journey, 2) Susan Barnett and Irene Prokop, two superb editors who were indispensable in making the manuscript clear and logical, 3) Elizabeth (Althea) Chadwick, for her recognizing and gifting the acronym ERA and her enthusiastic support of my work, and 4) Betty Wright and Betsy Lampe, the extraordinary women in the publishing business who made the book happen.

I hope each of you finds this product worthy of your efforts and your influence.

Permissions granted for:

- Excerpts from *Notes to Myself* © 1970 by Hugh Prather.
- Lyric excerpts from "Something That We Do" by Clint Black. Permission granted by Sussman & Associates.
- Excerpts from *Stanyan Street and Other Sorrows* by Rod McKuen, copyright 1954, 1960, 1961, 1962, 1963, 1964, 1965, 1966 by Rod McKuen. Used by permission of Random House, Inc.
- "Give Us This Day Our Daily Bread" and "What's Bugging You?" from *The Weeping Eye Can Never See* by Lois Wyse, copyright © 1972 by Lois Wyse. Used by permission of Random House Children's Books, a division of Random House, Inc.

- Excerpts from the preface of *Disarming the Past* © 1999 by Jerry M. Lewis, M.D.
- Excerpts from "Where Are You Hiding, My Love" from *There Are Men Too Gentle to Live Among Wolves* © 1970 by James Kavanaugh
- Excerpts from "On Marriage," from *The Prophet* by Kahlil Gibran, copyright 1923 by Kahlil Gibran and renewed 1951 by Administrators C.T.A. of Kahlil Gibran Estate and Mary G. Gibran. Used by permission of Alfred A. Knopf, a division of Random House, Inc.
- Excerpts from "If I Were A Poet," from *Times Alone: Selected Poems of Antonio Machado* © 1983. Published by Wesleyan University Press.
- Excerpts from *Knowing Woman, A Feminine Psychology* © 1990 by Irene Claremont De Castillijo, published by Shambhala Publications, Inc., Boston.
- Excerpts from Coleman Barks' *The Essential Rumi* © 2003.
- Lyric excerpt from *The Dance* by Tony Arata © Morganactive Songs, Inc. and EMI April Music Inc. All rights o/b/o EMI April Music Inc. administered by Morgan Music Group Inc. All Rights Reserved. Used by Permission. Warner Bros, Publications U.S. Inc., Miami, FL. 33014.
- Excerpts from "The Eternal Feminine" from *Writings in Time of War* by Pierre Teilhard de Chardin, translated by Reneè Hagues. Copyright © 1965 by Editions Bernard Grasset. English translation Copyright © 1968 by William Collins Sons & Co., Ltd., London and Harper & Row, Inc., New York. Originally published in French as Ecrits du Temps de la Guerre. Reprinted by permission of Georges Borchardt, Inc., for Editions Bernard Grasset.

Introduction

Why this book is for you and how to use it

"Love does not begin and end the way we seem
to think . . . love is a growing up."
                                        —James Baldwin

Each of us has our own special history of love relationships,
and we have learned how loving works because of that history.
Your most powerful lessons are those imprinted long ago—
perhaps so far back you have no conscious memory of them.
Piggybacked onto those childhood experiences are the romantic

encounters that came later. Beginning with your first falling-in-love experience and continuing right through to your most recent intimate relationship, the episodes have likely taken you from heaven to the edge of hell and back. All too often, a whiff of bliss is all you experience before disappointments creep in and disillusionment and power struggles begin. Though initially interspersed with periods of loving, passion, and good times, the bad times gradually take over until your dreams of "happily ever after" evaporate.

If this has been your experience, take heart. These repetitive, disappointing patterns do not have to dominate your relationships forever. All of us, through unhealthy models or traumatic events, have learned harmful lessons that have prevented us from creating lasting and fulfilling relationships. But be assured that the potential for lasting love burns bright within you. Claiming that potential will require you to learn more than your personal experience has taught you up to now. You will discover that it's not just that you haven't found "Mr. (or) Ms. Right," but that both you and your partner bring personal developmental issues into the relationship.

Turning the corner to claim your potential will take time, but know that you are not alone. Many are on the path to learning how to create healthy relationships, and many more are searching to find it. Until only a few years ago, I could certainly count myself among them. I'd yearned to have a deeply satisfying love relationship as far back as I could remember. And though I've given less revealing reasons—even to myself—for choosing the life work of psychologist and educator, I know that this yearning was part of my motivation. In searching for ways to help others toward the happily-ever-after I'd read about in fairy tales, I legitimized my own personal quest.

After several graduate degrees and two divorces, followed by twenty-five years as a single mom rearing three children, twelve years of teaching in universities, and over a third of a century in private practice, I have finally learned how to create with my husband, Sandy, a real-life happily-ever-after. A gratifying payoff is that I've helped hundreds of others create fulfilling, lasting love relationships as well.

Along the way, my experience as a licensed psychologist and marriage and family therapist (including twenty-plus years of training therapists), my working with Charles Truax as he devised models for Interpersonal Skills training, and my study and collaboration with Harville Hendrix in the development of Imago Relationship Therapy resulted in my creating *The New ERA of Intimacy* model. This model identifies natural forces that both initiate and eventually destroy a love relationship unless you redesign the way you communicate with your partner by incorporating ERA (Empathy, Respect and Authenticity). *Making Real Love Happen* shows you exactly how to bring about that redesign.

I have written this book for you. It contains the essence of a lifetime of learning about creating loving relationships. No matter how disheartened you may have become as a result of relationship disappointments or failures, you *can* have the relationship of your dreams—your sweet dreams, rather than your nightmares.

Although this book is a primer, the material is meaty. You may need to chew some pieces more than once. Other chunks may call for chipmunk treatment—store them in a side pocket of awareness for later. Moving beyond fairy tale notions will not be easy. New approaches are often suspect. In fact, you're almost certain to encounter some material that will be *so* suspect you won't even be willing to bite into it—much less chew or store it. Being open to considering information that flies in the face of what you think you know about yourself is, indeed, a challenge. The thought, *this doesn't apply to me*, can be a seductive alternative. So when you are tempted to say, "No way!" (or whatever fits when you emotionally discount something) go ahead and say it, re-open your mind, and continue.

Making real love happen is not easy, because healing from wounding experiences and becoming whole is not easy. Life has likely taught you this; if so, you have the scars on your heart to prove it. Happily, you are about to learn why this pursuit has been so difficult and what you can do to bring about the love you long for.

I *know* that the information and processes in this book are effective, and that they provide the path to both personal growth and committed relating. Growth occurs and results show up, as you actually do the work. I have seen it again and again—literally hundreds of times. But, as my grandmother used to say, "You will find the proof in the pudding." Or, as Einstein said, "Truth must stand the test of experience."

Accept the challenge to put it to the test. Two sections at the end of each chapter will help accomplish this challenge: *Make It Known* and *Make It Personal*. The *Make It Known* section recaps what you need to learn in order to understand why corrections need to be made, and the *Make It Personal* section specifies what to do to make the corrections.

Set apart a notebook that you will use exclusively for doing the work prescribed. Doing the exercises will cause you to both think in different ways and behave in different ways, making the otherwise theoretical and abstract, real and personal. And, by so doing, you will be on your way to *Making Real Love Happen*.

PART I

Understanding Relationship Dynamics

Human Nature Sets the Stage 1

Once upon a time

*B*ANG! THE GATEWAY FLINGS OPEN AND TWO hundred million sperm are released in a single explosion. What a race! Covering half an inch per minute, each spermatozoon frantically whips its tail in this swim for survival. Chances of success are poor, for only one swimmer will penetrate the ovum cell's surface and gain entrance. This wondrous event—a victorious sperm impregnating a human ovum—is your beginning. You, a tiny fertilized egg no larger than the point of a needle, have been conceived.

Within hours of conception, you begin growing and developing by dividing into like cells: two, then four, eight, and approximately nine months later, some 200 billion pulsing cells. A human infant, you stretch about twenty inches from head to toe and weigh some seven pounds.

And then you are born. The placenta, your source of nutrition during gestation, continues to feed you even as you leave the uterus and contend with the trauma of birth. But the placenta knows when you are on the outside, and pulsation through the umbilical cord ceases. The cord is severed. You are delivered from the relative *Shangri-la* of uterine life, from constantly available nourishment, comfort, protection and intimacy, into a new and unknown world.

At the time of your birth, you were among the most potentially resourceful and the most vulnerable of all living creatures. Picture yourself as a newborn infant. When you were in need, your only means of communicating discomfort were to tense your muscles, flail your arms and legs, and protest your misery with staccato cries.

The world into which you were so callously thrust was a poor substitute for the near-perfect home provided by your mother's womb. Often, in the new foreign environment, your needs went unmet. No matter how caring your caregivers were, they were simply not capable of meeting all your needs all the time. When you were hungry and the milk was not immediately available— one second late, one minute late, five minutes late—each time a need wasn't perfectly met, you experienced threat to your survival. Eventually, you learned to identify these perceived threats and the accompanying hurting feeling as *pain*.

Experiencing and dealing with pain in your world beyond the womb became a familiar challenge. As you grew, your needs for nourishment, comfort, and protection were continually frustrated. The agonizing reality of unmet needs and painful encounters persisted throughout your childhood and into adulthood—most likely, even up to this very moment. And I can imagine that if you were to look back over your life and identify your most painful encounters, you'd find they occurred and continue to occur within your intimate relationships. You can probably also identify with the fact that, whenever you are in pain, all your attention is drawn to the hurting, and you are consumed with making it go away.

It reminds me of an incident told me by a friend. Her mother had taken her automobile to the repair shop and asked that the car's brake-wear warning indicator be disconnected. When asked why, she replied, "Because seeing that red light upsets me."

The reaction of my friend's mother demonstrates a primitive human inclination: kill the messenger who brings bad news. We don't want to know when we're in danger. Feeling threatened is simply too frightening. So we numb our senses with a pill, more cherry pie, another drink, a bigger project, a new toy, a secret lover.

Yet, to be in danger and *not* be aware of it puts us in ultimate jeopardy. For example, people who are unfortunate enough to be born without sensory neurons (the messengers that communicate pain) have no way of sensing when something is wrong in their body. For them, even the simplest medical disorder can go undetected, leaving them vulnerable to complications and a potentially fatal outcome.

In exactly the same way, being unaware of *emotional* danger can place you in serious jeopardy. Not recognizing and addressing your psychological pain can condemn you to a lifetime of emptiness and unfulfilled promise. There are reasons why your heart feels like it's breaking when faced with the loss of romantic love. Do you know what it's like to feel as if you're falling apart or dying inside?

Granted, pain *is* painful, but it is also a fundamental survival mechanism; a blessing in disguise, so to speak. For the ability to experience pain in your body keeps you from being helplessly naive. Like the red light on the automobile dashboard, pain announces that something is wrong. It's a wake-up call—an alarm signal. To deny or ignore pain will inevitably exact consequences.

But even if you do suppress your pain, you are not left totally undefended, because your body automatically reacts in an attempt to correct or eliminate the threat. For example, when a child needs a parent's attention:

> Eight-year old Sam runs into the den, eager to tell his dad about his soccer game. Breathing hard, he says, "Dad, guess how many goals I scored?" And Dad, who has just plopped in his favorite chair after a hectic day at the office, says, "Not now, Son. I'm reading the paper. You can tell me about it later."
>
> "But, Dad!" The boy grimaces.
>
> "I said, 'Not now!' Go take a shower before dinner."
>
> Tension is building, and Sam knows from past experience that if he says anything else, his dad is likely to blow up. While temporarily successful in stopping himself, Sam feels like he's going to explode if he can't tell *somebody* about the game, and he really wants to tell

his dad. He scored three goals and he stole the ball from Joe Swanker *five* times! Opening his mouth to risk one last attempt, Sam sees his dad, looking up from under knitted brows, pointing his finger at him in that way that means, "If you say another word, you're going to get it!"

Sam's vocal chords freeze and his mouth closes. Eyes turned downward, he exits the den and follows his bowed head to his room. There, he flops chest-down on his bed, dirty uniform and all, and falls asleep.

Thirty minutes later, he's awakened by his mother's warm hand gently shaking his shoulder. "Dinner's getting cold," she whispers. That evening at the dinner table, nobody mentions the shower he didn't take and no one asks about the game. Sam picks at his meatloaf and chases a few peas and carrots around his plate. The only time he speaks is to mumble a request to be excused because he has a stomachache.

Sam didn't shut down because he *decided* to keep his news to himself. Rather, his impulse to reach out and express himself was thwarted because he "got it" deep in his gut that it would be too dangerous to spontaneously share his excitement. Sam's body reacted to the threat of his dad's exploding by shutting down awareness of his feelings.

The specific way that the body automatically reacts to pain is called *reactivity*. It truly is nature's way of trying to protect you from danger. When experiencing reactivity, your body shuts down feelings (like Sam's in this instance) or, in response to a different form of threat, exaggerates them.

Notice how well Sam's reactivity protected him. Given that the conscious urge to tell his dad about his athletic feats was gone, he wasn't tempted to try it. Thereby, he averted an immediate painful consequence.

However, this protection came with a price. Sam gave up a measure of conscious awareness of what he needed, and he gave up some of his natural spontaneity. Not a small price! Although nature's motive—keeping us alive—is clearly honorable, it's unfortunate that reactivity doesn't completely deliver on its intent.

We'll be exploring this concept of reactivity more fully later on, but for now it is enough to recognize that a reactive response is pre-programmed and automatic. The greater the threat causing the reactivity, the stronger the reactive response. As you learn to recognize reactivity and understand its purpose, you will also come to understand why you and your partner react the way you do with one another.

The *behavior* that emerges when we are reactive is programmed from childhood and is called *adaptive behavior*. We learn very early in life which behaviors reduce the danger of immediate punishment (or at least which ones protect us from *feeling* the pain when we are punished). The behaviors that were most effective in protecting us from immediate pain now occur automatically whenever we feel threatened.

Ironically, the behavior that we adopted when we felt unsafe may not have saved us at all. However, we tend to perceive events that occur immediately prior to a result as a cause-and-effect phenomenon. For example, if as infants we cried when we were hungry and the milk showed up, we learned that crying gets us milk. And human beings generalize. "Crying gets me milk" translates into: "Complaining causes others to give me what I want."

In Sam's case, his adaptive behaviors were both to suppress his feelings of excitement and to be quiet. These behaviors replaced his spontaneously sharing his exciting news. Somewhere down the line when Sam is older and more secure, he will need to reclaim his diminished awareness and his decreased spontaneity to become more fully alive and healthy. This won't be easy, for he'll have to risk allowing himself, once again, to feel his feelings of excitement and to express them openly. Because his past experience has programmed him to anticipate a punishing response to these behaviors, he'll be afraid to let himself go. We call this intentional process, of reinstating formerly disenfranchised behavior, *stretching*. Stretching activates the very fear that caused the shut down in the first place.

In other cases, such as a crying baby-turned-adult who learned that the only way to get her/his needs met was to complain loud enough and long enough, stretching will mean relaxing and giving up the excessive reaching out. S/he will have to release the unconscious belief that "if I don't *make* it happen, it *won't* happen." And, like in Sam's case, this will be difficult because it will activate the same fear that initially caused her/him to cry loudly and for a long time in the first place—nobody will come to feed me, and I'll die.

As you come to understand the dynamics of *pain, reactivity, adaptive behavior* and *stretching*, which are present in all significant relationships, you'll find yourself replacing your destructive, painful patterns with constructive ones. We're going to focus more on each of these; let's start with the attention-getter—pain.

Becoming aware of the nature of your physical makeup will help you understand what is happening in your body when you are in pain. (If this seems farfetched to you right now, no problem; the relevance will show up as we go along.)

You and everything else that exists in the entire universe, from the least amoeba to the largest galaxy, are created of units of electromagnetic energy called photons. These infinitesimally small bundles carry the energy of light, therefore—no science fiction here—you are truly a creature of light. Light is nothing more than electromagnetic waves—energy pulsing. The most dramatically evident characteristic of human beings, from the moment of conception throughout our lifetime, is the persistent pulsing motion within our cells and body.

Recognizing that your basic essence, like that of all nature, is *compacted pulsating energy* provides a powerful reality and imagery that can help you regain balance when you are feeling threatened. You can understand relationship issues, and especially *love* relationship issues, as never before once you comprehend the absolute, essential importance of the pulsing function. Anything that interferes with your pulsing is a threat of death; and, therefore, it is painful.

Imagine yourself—a mass composed of the billions of cells that make up your body—feeling relaxed. Then remember how you feel when you're stressed. When you sense that you are being closely controlled or manipulated, it's like being choked, crushed, smothered—like if you don't *get away from* the controlling force, you'll die. Or when your internal experience is that you are out of control, you feel as if you're disappearing into quicksand, terrified and desperate to *grab onto* something, anything, that you can hold onto. Both of these experiences are likely familiar to you, although one more than the other.

From now on, when you notice either of these, you can know that your pulsing is being interrupted, causing you to feel threatened. Like an engine out of tune, you will "run" roughly and inefficiently, causing stress, and resulting in excessive wear on your "parts." This painful interruption of your pulsing can occur only as the result of one of two provocations: either by your experiencing being intruded upon, or by your feeling excluded.

Intruding Relationship Behavior

Have you ever been in a relationship where you felt smothered—like if you didn't get away from it, you'd lose your individual identity? When you perceive another being *intrusive*— that is, being overbearing, smothering and controlling—you feel suppressed, suffocated, and desperate for space to be your own person doing what you want to do.

Intruding occurs as you experience that person exerting more than their share of influence in the relationship, leaving you without enough autonomy to express yourself freely and spontaneously. This experience of being intruded upon could result, for example, from your partner dominating a conversation and not allowing you equal time to express your thoughts and/or feelings.

Excluding Relationship Behavior

What about a relationship in which you felt ignored or neglected—like you weren't getting enough attention and/or connecting experiences? When you perceive that another person is *excluding*—that is, not spending enough time connecting with you—you feel shut out, devalued, and desperate to reconnect.

Excluding occurs as you experience another being unavailable and unresponsive unless you exert disproportionate energy and initiative to engage them. For example, you might feel excluded if your partner is engrossed in the newspaper. When you try to make conversation, s/he, without so much as looking up, responds with monosyllabic answers, if they respond at all.

When you and your partner are in conflict, whichever way your energy is being interfered with, your partner's energy is being interfered with in the opposite way. Every time. If you are feeling intruded upon, s/he will be feeling neglected and/or ignored, and vice versa.

Being reminded of two basic laws of physics will help you understand the reciprocity of interrupted pulsing. Simply stated,

1. Two objects cannot occupy the same space at the same time, and
2. Nature abhors a vacuum (void).

Therefore, in keeping with law 1, when one person's energy is expanding, the other's energy must constrict. And, in keeping with law 2, if the one is constricting, the other must expand to occupy the void being created.

When one partner is threatened, the other is threatened, although one is usually more aware of his/her emotional pain than the other. And every time you experience emotional pain, it's recorded in your body. Your body's record (memory) of pain is referred to as a *wound*. With ample wounding, you become chronically anxious and/or afraid, which adversely affects all aspects of your life—not the least of which are your intimate relationships.

Make It Known

1. The most dramatically evident characteristic of human beings, from the moment of our conception throughout our lifetime, is the persistent pulsing motion within our cells and body.

2. Each time one of your childhood needs was not perfectly gratified, your survival was threatened. Eventually, you learned to identify these perceived threats and the accompanying hurting feeling as *pain*.

3. Whenever pain is present in your body, your attention is drawn to the hurting, and making the hurting go away becomes a consuming focus.

4. Pain is a fundamental survival mechanism because it announces that something is wrong.

5. *Reactivity* is the specific way that your body innately and automatically reacts to pain in order to survive. The greater the threat causing the reactivity, the stronger the reactive response.

6. *Adaptive behavior* is the programmed behavior that you automatically exhibit when you are reactive. This behavior replaces the behavior that was discontinued because it was too dangerous.

7. *Stretching* is behaving in intentional ways that reclaim the discontinued behaviors that were too dangerous to maintain at an earlier time. Stretching is difficult because it reactivates the very fear that caused you to discontinue the behaviors in the first place.

8. Our basic essence is *compacted pulsating energy*. Anything that interferes with pulsing is a threat of death and causes pain. Maintaining balanced pulsing is paramount for staying alive and well.

9. The pulsing function can only be interrupted in one of two ways—by your being intruded upon or by your being excluded.

10. When you perceive another person being *intrusive*—that is, being overbearing, smothering, or controlling—you feel suppressed, suffocated, and desperate for space to be your own person doing your own thing.

11. When you perceive that another person is *excluding*—that is, not making sufficient connection with you—you feel shut out, devalued, and desperate to reconnect.

12. Whenever you and your partner are in conflict, one of you will need more togetherness (connection), and the other will need more freedom (space). If you are feeling neglected or ignored, s/he will feel intruded upon, and vice versa.

13. A *wound* is pain recorded in your body.

14. With ample wounding, you become chronically anxious and/ or afraid, which adversely affects all aspects of your life, including your intimate relationships.

Make It Personal

View a videotape (or visit an appropriate website) that shows actual frames of the beginning of human life. Two excellent historical videos you might view are:

- *The Miracle of Life*, produced by Swedish Television in association with WGBH in Boston in 1986. It won an Emmy Award in the highly acclaimed Nova Series that year.

- *Journey into Life; The Triumph of Creation.* Based on *The World of the Unborn*, produced in 1988, the video won an Academy Award Nomination for the Best Documentary Feature in 1990. It was made into a movie in 1992.

How Innate Reactions Impact Relationships

2

Into the deep woods

One mouth cannot discharge
All the venom of whole hate;
One heart cannot contain
All the richness of true love,
And so each thought and act affects
Not just you, but me.
Be careful what you do with us,
My dear, for
Hatred sours both our loaves,
And love makes rise the daily bread.

—Lois Wyse,
A Weeping Eye Can Never See (1972)

*N*OW THAT WE'VE EXPLORED PAIN IN SOME DETAIL,

let's look more closely at reactivity—the innate physiological reaction to pain that nature has provided as one of our survival mechanisms.

The form your internal reaction takes depends on how your pulsing is being interrupted—by intrusion or by exclusion. When you experience pain as the result of either of these phenomena, your body responds immediately and predictably. The two automatic, physiological responses are encoded in your reflex mechanisms; they are "instinctive." And the two forms are called *Minimizing* and *Maximizing*.

Minimizing

When you experience pain as resulting from the others' *intruding* on you, your reactive response is rigid *constricting*. In other words, when you experience the other person as expanding into your pulsing-out space—being bossy, pushy, demanding, overbearing, or excessively emotional—you *constrict* to become less open. This makes you less vulnerable to the intrusive other. You think your only sanctuary is in being alone. There, in your inner citadel, you can reassure yourself, "Yes, I am still here—intact." A descriptive picture of this state of mind is drawn in the words from a 60's Simon and Garfunkel song: "I am a rock . . . I am an island."

You've circled the wagons and kept out the deadly force. For your experience has taught you that the deadly force is the *other*. This internal urge to get away from the intrusive presence by constricting or shutting down is called *minimizing*. The fear that is driving you is that you will be overshadowed until your unique identity no longer exists.

For example, if a child perceives they are being bossed, constantly told what to do and what not to do, s/he may try to protect themselves from the watchful eye of the controlling caregiver by being out of sight and out of earshot. (This allows them to reclaim freedom to express their own preferences and choices.)

A nurturing parent who notices their child needing more freedom will set aside their own need to "fix the problem now," and give the child appropriate space. For instance:

Fourteen-year-old Christina shuts the front door behind her and heads for the refrigerator. Hearing the door close, her mother exits the study just in time to intercept her: "Hi, Honey. How was school today?"

"Fine."

"Did you get your test paper back in math?"

"Yeah."

"Well, how did you do?"

"I did fine, Mom."

"You did 'fine.' What does that mean? Did you make a 'C'?"

Christina is struggling. She's beginning to feel overwhelmed—like she wants to run away. It feels like she's been answering questions all day, and she needs a break. Her voice has an edge, "Mom, I already told you: Mrs. Jones doesn't give letter grades on weekly tests. She just puts down the number we got right." While attempting to maneuver around her mother without seeming rude, she hastily adds, "I'm really thirsty. I just want to get a Coke and call Jan before I have to go to basketball practice."

Stepping aside as Christina zigzags by, her mother is

not satisfied. Christina has really been having difficulty with math, and she's worried. But it's clear that her daughter doesn't want to talk about it right now.

"Okay. I'll be in the study if you need me."

This mother's decision, made regardless of her personal need to address the concern, was *not* elicited by her daughter's withholding, emotionally unavailable behavior. On this occasion, her respectful response was an expression of love, maturity and the desire to allow Christina freedom to have the discretionary time she needs between obligations. This doesn't mean that she won't reopen the discussion later, when Christina is not so pressed.

Conversely, if a parent is threatened by the adaptive behavior of the *minimizing* child, the parent will become reactive and be demanding, judgmental or controlling. In Christina's case, had her mother been threatened by her lack of responsiveness, she could have become controlling:

"Go ahead and get your Coke and bring it into the study. Calling Jan can wait. I want to see that math paper. We'll go over it and see if you know how to work the ones you missed. If you don't, we'll set aside a time to go over them together."

Such a scenario would have resulted in Christina's feeling more pressured, and she would have become less available, less flexible, and more remote. This reciprocal dynamic, minor as it may seem, could be damaging to both Christina and her mother by establishing or reinforcing a pattern of subtle abuse and control. And because the child is more dependent and vulnerable, her damage registers more deeply.

The more a painful dynamic such as this plays out, the more likely it will recur within the child's subsequent adult love relationships.

First of all, she will have been imprinted with an image of the only kind of person she believes can meet her survival needs: that person, when threatened, will tend to be overcontrolling, smothering, and/or excessively emotional. That is, someone inclined to *maximize*. And secondly, she will have learned to respond to feelings of being controlled or manipulated with *minimizing adaptive behavior*.

In essence, the child-turned-adult will have learned to behave in a way, when she is needy, that is *least* likely to evoke respectful behavior from her partner. And respectful behavior is what's most needed for her wounds from manipulation to be healed. Additionally, her adaptive behavior will re-wound her partner in his wounded places left over from childhood. Let's look at an example of how this might play out:

Natalie and Frank have been married five years. When Frank feels taken for granted, he becomes exasperated and then angry. His adaptive behavior is to get in Natalie's face and harp and nag.

Given that harping and nagging are intrusive, Natalie goes icy inside and shuts down connective feelings. Her adaptive behavior often begins with glaring and walking away from him.

Natalie is cooperating with nature's built-in way of protecting her from outside attack. Circle the wagons! Other minimizing behaviors she may exhibit are not answering him, displaying rigid facial expressions, and saying in a matter-of-fact, patronizing manner that his behavior is ridiculous. (Notice that he's getting *more* of what was painful to him in the first place—being ignored.)

Natalie's distancing (*minimizing*) adaptive behavior threatens Frank and increases his need to be noticed, so he becomes more belligerent. That is, the more Natalie attempts to shut him (the pain) out, the more he attempts to get her attention to alleviate his pain. Thus the destructive cycle repeats and escalates with each painful interaction.

The dynamic plays out something like this:

Frank booms, "Where'd this pillow come from! I've told you a thousand times—" Although maybe not "a thousand times," Frank has made this request repeatedly, in this same emotionally demanding manner. Part of Natalie's minimizing is refusing to "give in to his bullying."

Natalie—hearing the loud and critical tone, seeing the incensed eyes and twisted face, and feeling the anger spewing from his pores—goes cold and rigid inside, glares back at him, and walks out of the room.

Close on her heels, he continues booming his spiel: ". . . I don't want a pillow in *my* chair! Dammit! Can't you just for *once* listen to me and do what *I* want! There's not *one* chair in this whole damn house that —" Blah . . . blah . . . blah.

Finally, she turns abruptly, and in a measured and condescending tone, says, "Leave me alone! I am not going to talk to you until you stop acting like a raving maniac." And she strides out of the room, closing the door behind her. The fact that the door is closed with considerably more force than necessary belies her cool facade.

Natalie *constricted* because she perceived that Frank was being intrusive and she wanted to be less vulnerable in his presence. That is, she smelled the oncoming invasion of criticism, manipulation, and control, and sensed that her space to freely *be* was in jeopardy. The message Natalie heard from Frank is "I am the one here who has needs, and you should meet them." Resentment about the prospect of being conscripted caused her to create distance. The fear underlying the resentment was that Frank was going to control her and she would lose her identity, which was freedom to do things her way.

Sometimes intrusion can be experienced so subtly that we may hardly be aware that it's happening. Jack is an example of this:

Jack grew up sensing that he had to be a "good boy," which to him meant anticipating his parent's needs and expectations *before* they were stated, and then meeting them. Basically, he learned early to be overly responsible for meeting other people's needs while at the same time, suppressing his own.

In his teenage years, Jack's parents didn't give him a specific curfew, but he knew that his mother worried if he was out past 11:00 p.m. Therefore, he made every effort to be home by eleven so he wouldn't worry her—even if it meant that he left before the movie, party, or highlight of the evening was over. He took it upon himself to meet what he believed were his mother's expectations, regardless of whether or not they were spoken. Or in fact, regardless of whether they even existed.

Jack became hyper-vigilant in anticipating the needs of

significant others, and he felt obligated to personally ensure that the imagined needs were met. This sense of over-responsibility established a pattern of Jack feeling burdened in his primary relationships. It comes as no surprise that, as an adult, Jack struggles with commitment phobia. At his first inkling that a relationship is getting serious, he shuts down emotionally and is "out of there."

In other words, he *minimizes* to protect himself from being unconsciously obligated to meet the needs that he perceives in another. Staying distant and disconnected precludes his perceiving expectations, which is the only way he knows to protect himself from feeling obligated to meet them.

Because of Jack's history in intimate relationships, he is terrified by the unconscious burden of having to satisfy another's needs, while his own go unmet. Life has taught him the dysfunctional lesson that he can *not* maintain his individuality *and* be in a committed relationship. So he opts for the freedom to do his own thing at the expense of not having an intimate partner.

Maximizing

When pain is experienced as resulting from the other's remoteness or neglect (*excluding* behavior), your reactive response, like Frank in an earlier example, is to expand into the "space between." In other words, when you sense that nobody is there—they don't hear you, see you, or respond to you (they are deaf, blind, and dumb)—lifesaving behavior consists of your *making contact.*

For example, when a child calls out for his mother and she

doesn't answer, he calls again—this time louder. Still no answer. He runs around the house looking for Mother. The more time that passes with no Mother, the more threatened the child becomes. His adaptive behaviors are acts that are expansive, diffuse, demanding, and increasingly emotional.

Expanding is an attempt on the part of the child who perceives that he is disconnected and ignored to get the attention of the *constricting* or absent parent. His experience is that he feels not noticed, not seen, not heard, not valued. The parental message that he desperately needs to receive is "What you think, feel, and say is important to me. *You* are important to me!" Such a message would counter his fear of being abandoned and he could relax and play. The expanding reaction is referred to as *maximizing*.

So, nurturing parents reconnect when they notice that their child is needing attention. Let's look in on four-year-old Marsha and her mother, Sherry:

Marsha has a nine-month-old brother, Austin. Although she is a loving big sister, sometimes when Austin is requiring all of her mother's attention, Marsha feels left out.

On one particularly trying day, Austin had an earache. Inconsolable, he had been crying for hours. Consumed with trying to comfort him and start dinner at the same time, Sherry was startled by a loud bellow coming from behind her. She turned to see Marsha, lying on the pallet with one of Austin's baby bottles in her mouth, kicking her shoes into the floor and bawling as loudly as she could manage.

This was not a subtle message. Little Marsha was obviously feeling ignored, and she wanted attention right then!

Even though Sherry was exhausted from the day and still had dinner to prepare, she laid down the potato peeler and softly reached for this big, howling "baby" pounding on the floor. "Ooh, what a pretty baby! Does she have an earache? Let me put some warm drops in those little ears and rock her to sleep."

Straining to lift this gangly-legged "baby," Sherry cuddled Marsha in her arms, put some make-believe drops in her ears, and rocked her gently. Two or three minutes passed as Marsha pretended to be asleep in Sherry's lap, and then giggles burst forth as she jumped up protesting, "I'm no baby! I fooled Mommy! I fooled Mommy!" Jumping up and down with glee, she ran to get her little stool so she could help Mommy make dinner.

Having one more crying, demanding child was not the most endearing episode that Sherry could think of. Dinner still had to be made and she was already exhausted. However, her willingness to stretch into meeting her daughter's need for attention brought resolution in just a few minutes.

On the other hand, when a parent is threatened by the adaptive behavior of the *maximizing* child, she can become reactive and even more distant. Although Sherry loves both her children dearly, because she was tired and feeling pressed to prepare dinner, it would have been easy for her to have reacted by telling her little daughter coldly: "Get off that floor right now and hush that bawling! You're too old for that!"

Even if the parent gives in just to get some peace and quiet, the child often picks up on the resentment in the parent's effort, and knows that this is not connection. She may feel more devalued and therefore, angrier than ever.

The less available the parent is, the more terrified and expansive the child becomes. This reciprocal dynamic hurts *both* the child and the parent, and sets up a pattern of deprivation and fear. Because the child is the more dependent and vulnerable player, she is particularly damaged.

The more this painful dynamic plays out, the more likely it will manifest as a recurring dynamic within the child's subsequent adult love relationships.

First of all, she will have been imprinted with an image of the only kind of person she believes can meet her survival needs: a person who, when threatened, will tend to withdraw and be emotionally unavailable. That is, someone inclined to *minimize*. And secondly, she will have learned to respond to feelings of being ignored or neglected with *maximizing* adaptive behavior.

Let's see how maximizing behavior might be exhibited later down the line by looking in on a pair of newlyweds, Charles and Susan.

The wedding had been grand and the flight to their honeymoon destination had gone without a hitch. Their first night together in the Honeymoon Suite could not have been better. Now it's the next morning and Charles pops out of bed, eager to see the sights with his new bride. Susan, on the other hand, is still asleep.

Wanting to be thoughtful, he gently closes the bathroom door to muffle the sounds of shaving, showering, and blow drying. He takes his time grooming and slips on his favorite sweater and jeans. After sipping coffee and reading the morning paper on the balcony, he checks on Susan again. Still sleeping.

Charles is hungry. It's almost eight and he usually eats at six-thirty. Besides, he's getting impatient. And lonely. He wants Susan's company.

Sitting on the edge of the bed, he kisses her gently and whispers, "Wake up, Mrs. Jacobs. Mr. Jacobs would like to treat you to the ultimate breakfast—anything you want." Eyes still closed, Susan mumbles something about trying to sleep, and rolls away from him, pulling the covers over her exposed shoulder.

Although disappointed, Charles is feeling affectionate, and he wants to take good care of his new bride. Putting his hand on the covered shoulder, he shakes her gently and says, "I'll leave a wake-up call for an hour from now, and meet you at the coffee shop downstairs at ten. I'll go ahead and order for us, so you can just show up and your breakfast will be right there waiting for you." Feeling pleased with himself for displaying such unselfish thoughtfulness, he pats the biggest curve under the blanket and lets himself out.

Susan's gut tightens vaguely as, adjusting from her right side to her left, she drifts back to sleep.

It's 10:00 a.m. Charles smiles as he sips even more hot coffee. Breakfast for two has arrived on time. He looks expectantly toward the coffee shop entrance, sure that Susan will appear any moment now.

Ten thirty-one a.m. A second three cups of coffee later. Still no Susan. By now, Charles is angry. (Because he is feeling neglected and/or abandoned, he is *maximizing*).

Let's listen in on his thoughts:

"Where is she? I can't believe she's not here! Breakfast

. . . cold . . . ruined. I've wasted my entire morning waiting for her. This is our honeymoon. And she wants to sleep?! I've tried really hard to be thoughtful. I've done everything I could think of to make things perfect for her. I should have gone ahead and eaten an hour ago like I wanted to rather than drown myself in damn coffee.

"Hold on! Maybe something's happened to her. What if she had a heart attack? Wait! Did I lock the door? Someone could have raped her! He could be up there right now!"

Frantic, Charles bolts from the table laden with cold, undisturbed food, and not wasting time waiting for an elevator, races up the stairs. Shaking as he crams the card key into the electronic lock, he hurls the door open, and there—right where he left her over an hour and a half ago, curled up and slightly snoring—is Susan.

Grabbing her shoulders and shaking them, he blurts out, "Are you all right? Where were you?" Susan's eyes pop open. Startled and somewhat disoriented, she gazes at him through blurry eyes. "What's wrong?"

Although less loud, the accusing tone persists: "You scared me to death. Didn't you get the wake-up call?" Not pausing for an answer, he continues, "I ordered breakfast and sat there waiting for you for an hour. I thought something horrible had happened to you!"

A fly on the wall notices Susan's shoulders hunching and narrowing as she shrinks back into the rumpled sheets.

How did this scene come about?

The potential for discord presents any time two people, especially two people in an intimate relationship, don't want the same thing. In this case, Charles was ready to get up and Susan wanted to sleep in. Seems like no big deal. Still basking in the afterglow from their first night together as newlyweds, each happily went with what felt natural. However, in a few short hours, what felt natural resulted in a situation that proved painful for both.

The dynamic worked like this: Charles was frustrated. This is not the way he had expected their first morning to go, so he took charge, regrouped, and made a plan. He decided to be thoughtful and let Susan sleep another hour before meeting him in the coffee shop downstairs. He was pleased with himself. He had overcome being disappointed that Susan was not ready to jump out of bed and see the sights with him, and he had gotten everything back on track.

When he told Susan the plan for *their* morning, however, her gut tightened. That her body reacted by constricting evidences that Susan perceived, even if at an unconscious level, that his plan was intrusive. He had taken control and made decisions for both of them. (Unbeknown to Susan, she was ignoring *his* needs by continuing to sleep.)

Reactivity escalated in the next round. Susan slept (minimized) beyond her wake-up call which left Charles feeling even more neglected and taken for granted. Therefore he *maximized* by getting angry, then frantic. He expressed his escalating emotions by bolting into the room, making demands, and shaking and berating Susan.

These behaviors were Charles's attempt to get his need for attention met. Notice, however, that is *not* what he got. Rather, for the second time, Susan experienced his *maximizing* behavior as intrusive, so once again, she *minimized*—as evidenced by her body's hunching, narrowing, and shrinking back. Of course the more Susan withdrew to avoid being controlled, the more intensely Charles advanced to try to stay connected. That this destructive cycle is self-perpetuating is obvious. The honeymoon was just beginning and the Power Struggle had already begun. And the cycle will sporadically escalate throughout their relationship until both Susan and Charles learn to meet one another's needs, Susan must honor Charles's need for attention and connection, and Charles must honor Susan's need for space to do her own thing.

Sometimes it's hard to see how you might have been damaged by neglect. I remember particularly one client who was adamant that she could not possibly have been neglected because she had such a loving mother. Her story came out gradually over several sessions. This is a summary of the traumatic early childhood experiences that she resurrected. Her name is Greta.

Born in Berlin, Germany, in November of 1944, Greta never knew her father, a brave captain in the *Luftwaffe,* who last contacted her mother in early August 1944. It was presumed that he was killed in battle.

That winter, Greta's mother was forced to turn to the streets to rummage for food. Every morning, just after dawn, she carefully secured her bundled baby with knotted strips of blanket to a two-wheeled wooden cart that was never far from her side as she scavenged. The rubble that had replaced the once well-tended streets of Berlin hardly facilitated passage on foot, much less by rickety cart. Unfortunately, Greta's everyday exposure to the sounds, smells, sights, and terrors of war was exacerbated by unattended periods when no mother's face was visible to soothe her fears, and no comforting, soft body muted the deafening booms that rocked her world. (She was experiencing neglect, albeit, *not* from a neglectful mother.) No matter how strong her mother's desire and will to keep her baby comfortable, nurtured, and safe—which was considerable—life circumstances limited her ability to do so.

As a young and beautiful woman, Greta migrated to the United States. When she entered therapy with me, her goal was to have a permanent, loving relationship. She reported that in two former marriages, as well as in several almost-marriages, each man left her voicing these complaints:

"No matter how much attention I give you, it's never enough."
"You smother me."
"You're too possessive."

(You'll recognize these as complaints made by someone who is experiencing being intruded upon.)

Her *maximizing adaptive behavior* had consistently created the self-fulfilling prophecy that she most feared—abandonment! One person feels smothered and leaves; both partners lose.

In essence, the neglected child-turned-adult will have learned to behave in ways, when she is needy, that is *least* likely to evoke connecting behavior from her partner. And connecting behavior is what's most needed for her wounds from being abandoned, to heal. Additionally, her adaptive behavior will re-wound her partner in his vulnerable places left over from childhood.

These dynamics of minimizing and maximizing have a huge impact on relationships. Can you identify with this dynamic in your present and/or past relationships? Are you typically the *minimizing* or the *maximizing* partner? Even though no one always minimizes or always maximizes (because the form of your reactivity depends on how you're being threatened), you do have a primary reactive style.

Your primary reactive style is the one that you experienced most often and most intensely when you were a child. Therefore, that becomes the reactive style that you will generalize when you can't clearly distinguish the nature of a threat. Note that, contrary to popular belief, these styles are *not* gender specific.

As you come to understand the dynamics of reactivity, you will see how (1) a person whose primary adaptive style is maximizing, is always attracted to someone whose primary adaptive style is minimizing. And (2) a person whose primary adaptive style is minimizing, is always attracted to someone whose primary adaptive style is maximizing. This is predictable, and it sets up a destructive cycle of partners wounding and re-wounding one another. Chapter 4 will explain this phenomenon in detail so that you can learn how to move from a lose/lose pattern into a win/win pattern.

The more wounds you acquire, the more anxious and fearful you become. Anticipating pain, or being afraid, is in itself painful. Therefore, when you are anxious or afraid you become reactive, and the form of your *reactivity* depends on your experience-based expectation. If life has taught you that you are about to be intruded upon, you will *constrict* and become rigid, unavailable, unresponsive, emotionally cold and/or hyperrational. You will *minimize*.

On the other hand, if you believe you are going to be shut out, you will become diffuse, demanding, and excessively emotional. You will *maximize*. Recall that when you are reactive, you create a threatening context for the other. You are literally doing all you can to elicit from the other the exact behavior that you fear. In other words, you're creating a self-fulfilling relationship prophecy. After you've learned to be anxious and fearful, you become an active force in recreating your own painful past, or prison, which causes more pain with partners, resulting in more wounds, resulting in more anxiety and fear, etc.

The destructive cycle continues as you plummet throughout life—the poor get poorer—unless the learned adaptive pattern is consciously and purposely interrupted.

By intentionally becoming more self-aware, you can learn to recognize your internal feelings of reactivity. Eventually you will be able to readily identify when you're *minimizing* in response to your being denied the room you need to express yourself, as well as when you're *maximizing* in response to your not getting the contact you desperately need. You can also cultivate the awareness that your partner will be living the complementary phenomenon—that is, if your feelings are shutting down or if they are escalating, you will know that your partners' feelings will be the opposite. Your experience will drive home the reality that one exacerbates the other.

Altering this seemingly hopeless scenario *is* possible. But you will not be able to make it happen by following your instincts. Rather, you must intentionally change the very behaviors that have become second nature to you. And though every fiber of your being will resist, if you are to break out of the grip of your entrenched defense, you must do it anyway.

A personal example may help to illustrate this point. As far back as I can remember, if I was really interested in a boy, I was afraid to let anyone know—especially the boy himself!

> I had a crush on this super-cute guy in high school. He was co-captain of the football and basketball teams, funny, and really smart in math. But every time I saw him in the hall or at a game, I avoided him. When he started going steady, I was brokenhearted.
>
> Forty-three years later at our 40th High School Class Reunion he told me he'd secretly had a crush on me all through high school, but he'd thought I didn't like him.

If only I'd been able to overcome my fear and stretch into letting my feelings show a little, perhaps life would have been more fun back then. But I didn't and the pattern continued.

For years of my adult life I avoided men that I was attracted to. I guess I was afraid that they wouldn't be attracted to me. Therefore—no surprise here—only rather aggressive men came into my life. I was well into my early fifties when I began intentionally changing this adaptive behavior of distancing. By then, being authentic was really scary and I was really inept. The first few times I practiced being more open, I think I overdid it. (By the way, I've discovered that this is to be expected. When we're out-of-balance in one direction, shifting from that will catapult you into being almost as out-of-balance in the opposite direction.) The men must have been as embarrassed as I was—they never called back. But I improved. Fortunately, when my natural *minimizing* reactions occur with my husband, Sandy, I am much more capable of countering my inclinations and, instead, I consciously reach out in a more balanced manner.

Mark, the subject of our next example, is also learning to stretch. He, however, is challenged to counter his *maximizing* responses.

Mark is very possessive in his relationship with his wife, Jan. A review of his dating history bears evidence that this is a long-standing pattern. Though he reports never thinking of himself as domineering or controlling in his relationships, he does admit to being jealous.

The first time Jan and Mark came into my office for marriage counseling, Jan reported that she felt smothered in their relationship: "Anytime I want to go anywhere when he's home, he has to go with me. Otherwise, he's uncomfortable and nervous the whole time I'm gone. And I pay for it in one way or another— usually by his being cranky the rest of the day."

Mark agrees that this is true. His comment in response is, "I work five days a week. If you really wanted to be with me, you'd get your running around done while I'm at work. I think you're being selfish and inconsiderate of my feelings when you go off and leave me alone. We have too little time together as it is."

Through learning about the minimizing and maximizing dynamic, Jan and Mark have learned to be more responsive to each other's needs. Mark has discovered that the more sensitive he is to Jan's need to have time to herself, the less she feels the need to be away from him. Because Mark now respects Jan's need for a sense of autonomy from time to time, he frequently suggests that she go shopping, have lunch with a friend, or whatever strikes her fancy. (Jan, of course, has her lessons to learn about meeting Mark's needs for attention and connection.)

By choosing to intentionally alter self-defeating adaptive behavior, you *can* break the destructive cycle. If you are automatically constricting, reach out, let your partner feel that you are present and interested. If you are automatically intruding, let go! Give your partner room to breathe.

Shifting the expression of your energy is essential; balanced pulsing must be restored within both you and your partner. However, stretching beyond your natural reactive response, and selecting to alter self-defeating adaptive behavior, isn't easy to do. And it isn't easy for many reasons.

First of all, it won't be easy because it won't *feel right*—and because it doesn't feel right, you can't believe it *is* right. Your historic experience has taught you how to behave when your needs are not being met, and it is extremely difficult to break old patterns. Also, you won't be adept in the new behavior, which will initially increase the likelihood that you will be criticized and rejected, just as you feared.

As if these reasons weren't enough, your internal struggle is compounded further: Because you have been doing everything you know to do to get what you want and it hasn't worked, you can't make sense of what's happening. "Cognitive dissonance"—the psychological term for this mental state will not be tolerated for long. You can't abide feeling crazy. So you'll make up ways to understand why your world is working as it is: "I haven't found the *right one*," "I must really be screwed up," or "Maybe real love just doesn't exist in the real world." These and other common rationalizations can soothe the internal dissonance and provide excuses that allow you to give up on the relationship.

Your rationalizations are not plucked out of thin air. Chapter 3 will provide clues to the source of their origins.

Make It Known

1. *Reactivity* takes one of two forms depending on the cause of the inflicting pain:

   a. *Minimizing*, when the inflicted pain is caused by the perception that the other is attempting or planning an invasion of control and manipulation.

   b. *Maximizing*, when the inflicted pain is caused by the perception that the other is unavailable or unresponsive.

2. No one always minimizes or always maximizes; the form of the reactivity depends on how you're being threatened. But you do have a *primary* reactive style, which is the one that you experienced most often and most intensely when you were a child. This becomes the reactive style that you will generalize when you can't clearly distinguish the nature of a threat. These styles are *not* gender specific.

3. The dynamic of reactivity sets up and perpetuates the re-wounding cycle, given that those with primary *minimizing* styles are always attracted to those with primary *maximizing* styles, and vice versa. Every couple that falls in love consists of two people who have opposite primary reactive styles. That's because they will have experienced their greatest pain from being wounded in different ways—one by being manipulated and/or controlled; the other by being neglected and/or abandoned.

   a. When threatened, the partner whose major wounds resulted from being manipulated and/or controlled, needs space to be their own person. When the partner primarily needing connection notices the other's attempts to get the space he needs, she will perceive his actions as withdrawing, and will feel shut out.

b. When threatened, the partner whose major wounds resulted from being neglected and abandoned, will need closeness and connection. Their partner primarily needs space. When the partner primarily needing space notices the other's attempts to engage him, he will feel manipulated, controlled, and intruded upon.

4. The more you are wounded, the more anxious and fearful you become. When you are anxious or afraid, you are in a reactive mode and will automatically engage in adaptive behavior.

5. The automatic adaptive behavior of one partner will threaten the other, which results in their being re-wounded.

6. By choosing to intentionally alter self-defeating adaptive behavior, you can break the destructive cycle of re-wounding. If you are automatically constricting, you will need to stretch into reaching out. If you are automatically intruding, you will need to stretch into letting go.

Make It Personal

1. As best you can recall from your growing-up years, make a list of the major complaints that you had of caregivers (parent-figures). Be sure to include what they did and did not do that was most frustrating to you.

2. What form did your reactivity typically take in response to these frustrating experiences, *minimizing* or *maximizing*? How do you remember feeling?

3. What were some of the adaptive behaviors that you exhibited when you were reactive?

4. Does this pattern repeat itself within meaningful relationships in your present life?

5. What is your primary stretch challenge—reaching out or letting go?

6. Fill in the blank: My primary reactive style is

_____.

Lessons Learned In Childhood 3

Enter the wicked witch

I know your eyes do not answer mine,
They look and do not question when they look.
Your clear eyes, your eyes have the calm
 and good light,
The good light of the blossoming world, that I saw
One day from the arms of my mother.
> —Antonio Machado (1875-1939),
> "If I Were A Poet,"
> *Times Alone* (1983)

STORIES PLAY A MAJOR ROLE IN OUR LEARNING HOW
the world works and why it works that way. When you were a

child, bedtime stories, religious parables, dramas acted out in the media, and/or anecdotes lived in your presence were powerful influences that shaped your value system and rationale for decision-making.

Fairy tales play a particularly dramatic role in forming our early beliefs regarding love relationships. In the fall of 1999, front-page headlines of major newspapers reported an Associated Press story addressing the shocking statistics showing that no U.S. region has a higher divorce rate than the Bible Belt:

> ". . . In a country where nearly half of all marriages break up, divorce rates in these conservative states are about 50 percent above the national average.
>
> "Aside from the quickie-divorce mecca of Nevada . . . Tennessee, Arkansas, Alabama and Oklahoma round out the Top Five in the frequency of divorce."
>
> The author, David Crary, quotes some of the explanations offered: "Kids don't have a very realistic view of marriage . . . they have flawed models around them. . . . Fundamentalist churchgoers are often exposed to 'fairy tale conceptions of marriage. . . .'"

Society's mindset is permeated by fairy tale messages about how love comes into our lives. Let's explore this impact by listening with our eyes to a well-known fairy tale, one that I remember from my childhood. Perhaps you remember it too. Though your story and personal challenges are appreciably unique, you may be surprised to notice that they are remarkably similar—at least in the beginning—to the scenes in *Rapunzel*. Fairy tales engage childlike imaginations and create expectations that can influence us throughout our lives—without our ever being aware of it.

Many versions of Grimms' fairy tale *Rapunzel* exist, but I've taken liberty to recount the fairy tale as it was told to me. It is the story of a beautiful young maiden who was imprisoned in the castle tower by the Wicked Witch.

. . .The craggy-faced, snaggle-toothed, wrinkled old Witch taunted fair Rapunzel day after day—"You're as ugly as I am, Rapunzel! You're as ugly as I am!" After a time, the taunting became Rapunzel's truth. She *believed* herself ugly—as ugly as the Wicked Witch.

One day a handsome Prince, while riding through the forest, heard a reminiscent haunting melody gently pealing through the morning mist. The clear tones were unmistakably those of a pure, young maiden. Following the music led him deeper into the woods where he came upon an abandoned castle. The melodious notes wafted from above, and as his eyes climbed the encrusted stone walls, he saw—through the highest tower window—a fair maiden singing as she brushed her long blond hair. He was enchanted by Rapunzel's innocent beauty and implored her to *let down her hair* so that he could gain entrance to her prison and set her free. Taken by his strikingly handsome countenance and compassionate voice, Rapunzel reluctantly lowered her hair from the open window, all the while fearing that, as he drew close, this handsome young man would see her true ugliness and be repulsed.

What happened instead was beyond her fondest imaginings. As he climbed through the open window and their glistening eyes met, she saw reflected a most beautiful creature gazing back at her. To her utter astonishment, she slowly recognized the radiant stranger in the reflection—it was *herself*!

At first, the words came out slowly and incredulously . . . "I am . . . beau . . . ti . . . ful!"; then with more conviction: "I am . . . beautiful!" The words began to tumble about like a lyric to a long-forgotten melody inside herself. And as the melody gained momentum, along with the momentum came the recognition that she really was not ugly like the Wicked Witch.

With that recognition, the Witch's spell was broken. Rapunzel was free to claim her beauty *and* her Prince. And they

lived happily ever after.

Why did Rapunzel believe she was ugly? Because the Wicked Witch, who was the major influence in her life, *told* her she was ugly. Who would want to be around someone so ugly as she? What kept her from having what she so desperately needed—companionship and love—was her own ugliness.

Like Rapunzel, you too have received messages about yourself. Ever since your receptors were well enough developed to "receive," you've been impacted by your environment. And you've personalized these experiences. The immature functioning of a young child's mind operates with the central assumption that "whatever is happening, I am causing." When something happened that caused you pain (even an occasion as simple as wanting something and not getting it), you reasoned that it was your fault. Whether accurate or not, you've internalized these negative childhood messages and believe them to be true.

For instance, imagine the child who is sexually abused. Who

among us would presume that a small child is responsible for being violated in this most intimate way? Certainly no grownup in their right mind. Yet, time and again, while working with adults who have been abused in this way, what eventually and inevitably surfaces is guilt and shame that's been buried from all those years ago. I've heard many a story from troubled hearts remembering themselves as a child lying in their little bed at night—terrified that the door would open—trying to figure out what bad thing they had done that was making their mommy/daddy/grandfather/brother/etc. do this to them.

Being sexually abused, particularly by someone who is supposed to be a trusted caregiver, is intensely traumatic; therefore, the child reasons, "I must be really bad to deserve to be treated this way." Such thinking results in their blaming themselves for being abused: "A bad person like me deserves to be abused," and they come to hate the Self within that "causes" their pain. And the more pain they experience, the larger their pool of self-hatred becomes.

This story will touch the reality of many. And others of you, about now, may be saying to yourself, "Well, if this is the way a child reasons, I can see how someone who was sexually abused could have a pool of self-hatred." But the truth is, this dynamic plays out for all of us, even you.

"But I wasn't sexually abused," you may be thinking. "I had good parents and a happy childhood—or reasonably so. I couldn't possibly hate myself. Maybe I have twinges of feeling unworthy here and there, but I certainly don't *hate* myself."

Recall my mentioning earlier that none of us had a childhood wherein all our needs were met perfectly all the time. And since we unconsciously blame ourselves for our pain, at least some self-hatred is stored in everyone. All of us who have major difficulties in intimate relationships have had enough painful experiences to produce a pool of self-hatred. And the deeper the pool, the more reactive we are.

Just mentioning the possibility that you have such a repository may elicit reactivity within you. If you too quickly (denying before you have even had time to think about it) respond to the suggestion with: "No way! Not me. I couldn't possibly hate myself," you are likely being defensive. The other reactive style is, of course, to become overly emotional—perhaps angry: "This is B.S.!" Most of us are not aware that our own self-hatred is keeping us from becoming a happy person in a healthy relationship.

That some have more self-hatred than others is evident. It seems logical that the more deprived a person has been by life circumstances, the more self-hatred s/he will harbor and the less happy and capable of having a healthy relationship s/he will be. However, it turns out not to work quite as simply as that. Some people who have experienced major deprivation become happier and have more fulfilling intimate relationships than others who have undergone relatively minor episodes of having their needs frustrated. How could this be?

One of the finest professors I had in graduate school, Dr. Merl Bonney—who was renowned for his lifelong research and study of differences between "High Normals," (well-adjusted people), and "Low Normals" (poorly adjusted people)—taught me about this complex phenomenon. I remember one morning as clearly as if I were sitting there—second seat, third row—right now:

> Ranting on about the misfortunes revealed by his research subjects that morning, Dr. Bonney characteristically had his single-digit forefinger shaking in the air. "I never heard such a damn outpouring of foul circumstances! My God, everybody had at least one divorce. Some were

orphaned or abandoned as kids," head shaking in disbelief. "One guy was paralyzed, in a wheel chair. . . ." His animation peaked as he concluded, "No wonder these people are so screwed up!"

Pause.

"Then," thoughtfully, "the damnedest thing happened: I realized I had been talkin' to High Normals all morning."

A puzzled look preoccupied him for the longest time. Then the bell rang.

A major conclusion drawn by Bonney's research is that life circumstances do not differentiate between generally well-adjusted and happy people versus generally maladjusted and unhappy people. Rather, the difference is in what people *do* with their life circumstances. So the fact that you do not always get your needs met—particularly when you are beyond childhood—does not in itself cause you to live an unhappy life without a fulfilling intimate relationship. "My childhood made me do it" is mostly the rationalizing of an unaware person who is choosing to live his/ her life as a victim—not a cause that can't be overcome.

However, this doesn't mean that you become well adjusted or not, all on your own. We are, by our very nature, relational and interdependent creatures, which means that we affect and are affected by everyone around us. And the closer the association, the greater the effect. Therefore, if you get strong negative messages from those close to you, you are likely to become trapped in the prison of self-hatred.

Your deciding vote, as an adult, in being able to lessen your self-hatred is in the way you learn to understand your life (the life story you create), and in the selection of whom to be around (particularly, whom to be close to). Looking back on your history, can you identify people in whose presence you have felt bad about yourself? People who have brought you down? If you allow yourself to be with those who blame, shame, and criticize, that is, those who are projecting their own self-hatred, you will most likely learn to hate yourself. Whether they are critical of themselves, of you, or of others, is relatively immaterial. These are people to stay away from as much as possible. Otherwise, by being influenced by them—and you cannot avoid being influenced by those around you—you learn that "I'm as ugly as you are."

Self-hatred is symbolized in the fairy tale *Rapunzel* as the "Wicked Witch." To protect us from consciously seeing *ourselves* as the "Wicked Witch," we create an ugly, wicked witch *outside* ourselves. "Since I'm in this stinking prison, somebody has to be at fault!" To prevent our consciously believing *we* are the guilty party, we delude ourselves into believing that the fault is in the "other." Our unconscious reasoning concludes: "Since you and I are the only ones here, and I can't allow it to be my fault that I'm in this mess, *you* must be the culprit!" And the negative feelings toward the identified enemy, along with the blaming and shaming criticism, begin. Once we are infected with this contagious virus, we pass it back and forth, and with each pass, both parties hate themselves and the other more.

This dynamic of seeing in someone else what would be too painful for us to see in ourselves is a form of *projection*. *Projection* is when you see another as though s/he is a mirror that reflects a part of yourself; that is, you see in *them* what is really in *you*. In the words of *The Talmud*: "We do not see things as they are; we see things as *we* are."

For an example of projection in operation, listen in on an interaction between Evelyn and Jake:

Evelyn: "You always think I'm looking at other men. I can't believe how jealous you are, and you have absolutely no reason to be."

Jake: "Evelyn, that is just not true. You're the one who accuses *me* of flirting with other women when we're out."

Jake is, in fact, not jealous. In this case, it *is* Evelyn who is the jealous one. But her tendency to flirt and have mental affairs is incongruent with her value system and her self-image, so she must keep herself from realizing that she does this "bad" thing. Transferring the trait onto Jake by convincing herself that *he* is the jealous one, acknowledges the dynamic in their relationship— it just misrepresents the source.

An example of Jake's projecting onto Evelyn shows up in this interaction:

Evelyn: "I'd like to be included when you entertain clients at least every now and then. I really feel left out because you never invite me to come along."

Jake: "I don't invite you because I never know what kind of mood you're going to be in, and I don't want to be embarrassed in front of my clients by your snide remarks."

In this instance, Jake *is* projecting onto Evelyn. She is not inclined to take verbal potshots at him. Rather, it's Jake who may well make disrespectful comments about Evelyn when he's in a negative frame of mind. So he is projecting his inclination to criticize her in public (which is incongruent with his value system) onto her. He believes that she's the one who exhibits the "bad" behavior, because it's too threatening to recognize it in himself.

This unconscious technique of projection is omnipresent in relationship impasses. It is nature's attempt to protect you from being consciously aware of the things that you hate about yourself. To be conscious of these parts of yourself that are in conflict with your value system would be devastating. You cannot abide your own self-hatred.

So for projection to protect you, it must go on at an unconscious level. You're not aware that you're blaming yourself for your pain. You're not aware that you hate the parts of your Self that you have identified as being responsible for your disadvantaged state. You're not aware that what you hate in another really lives denied and disowned in your self. *"You're as ugly as I am!"*

Just as self-hatred is the core cause of negative projections, it is also the core cause of criticism. This becomes evident as you recognize that *every criticism is projection.*

Any message, when delivered with a harshly critical spirit, is a partially conscious, partially unconscious communication, because *all criticism is adaptive behavior born in reactivity.* Think of criticism or critical spirit as anything you say, do, think, or feel while focusing on fault. It can manifest in the form of a thought, a look, a gesture, a posturing of the body, a verbal tone, an act, or an utterance.

Consider that "constructive criticism" is an oxymoron. Criticism is never beneficial—either to the giver or to the receiver. Consider, instead, the gift of discernment. You and I can differentiate between criticizing and discerning, we can "feel" the difference. With criticism, we can actually sense stress (an imbalance of our pulsing) regardless of whether we are the one doing the criticizing or the one being criticized. To *discern* is to recognize as separate and different, perhaps to contrast our reality with our perception of another's reality. No judgment of better-than/worse-than exists, and none is necessary for clear boundary setting. Neither criticism nor projection is a part of discernment. In fact, becoming more discerning is part of becoming more mature.

> For example: As Dave is driving Cheryl home from a movie, he removes a cigarette from his shirt pocket and engages the car lighter. Interrupting their lively discussion, she respectfully says, "Dave, one of the things I may not have told you about myself is that I get headaches when I'm confined in a small space with cigarette smoke. I realize this is an imposition, but I would really appreciate your not smoking until we're out of the car."
>
> "Hey, no problem," Dave replies. "Thanks for telling me."
>
> The unlit cigarette slides back into his pocket as their conversation resumes.

Notice how smoothly the communication between Cheryl and Dave went. The two clearly have opposing needs, which were expressed. Yet each honored the other in a mutually respectful manner.

On the other hand, to *criticize* has a hierarchical, arrogant flair of disrespect for the other that communicates, "I am more important than you" or "I know better than you." For an example of how criticism might have played out in the interaction between Dave and Cheryl, let's go back to Dave engaging the car lighter.

Alerted to the realization that he is about to smoke, Cheryl tenses and turns away. Rolling her window down, she positions her nose in the direction of the open space and goes silent as Dave smokes his cigarette. When they park in her driveway, Cheryl immediately opens her door and gets out of the car, fanning her frowning face with her hand. Dave is nervous. He isn't sure what's wrong but he feels as though Cheryl doesn't want to be with him. The evening that had been going so well has somehow turned sour.

Interactions that include discernment are win/win. Interactions that include criticism are lose/lose.

Criticizing is an adaptive behavior that you resort to when you're trying to make others treat you better so you'll feel better. Does it work? Hardly! It is not only woefully inadequate; it is counterproductive and sets up a vicious cycle. Every time you criticize your partner, you're projecting your self-hatred onto her/him. And the outcome is predictable. As s/he feels criticized and hurt, s/he will project her/his own self- hatred onto you. You will literally be programming your partner to repeat the very behaviors that hurt you in the first place. And of course, you've set her/him up for the same dynamic.

The cycle perpetuates itself, making it increasingly difficult for you to learn to love—either to learn to love yourself, or to learn to love another. And it's the most you can do to influence your partner to be less lovable and less capable of loving you.

It is this spirit of criticism that keeps us stuck—that keeps us imprisoned. A critical spirit is the poisonous outpouring from our cesspool of self-hatred. And it contaminates all it touches.

If something that you do rankles me
I can know that your fault is my fault too.
The criticism that hurts the most is the
one that echoes my own self-condemnation.

—Hugh Prather, (1970) *Notes to Myself*

You can begin to comprehend how you become imprisoned in a life of remote loneliness and unhappiness as you understand (1) the reciprocal dynamic between minimizing reactivity and maximizing reactivity, and (2) the role that self-hatred plays in the projection of criticism.

The prison of self-hatred, once entered, is inescapable on your own. Like Rapunzel—once you come under the influence of self-hatred (the Wicked Witch), you become a victim. Rapunzel could not escape her tower prison by herself, because there was no door. There were no stairs. At the same time, the Handsome Prince—even though he was a prince—could not save her by himself. He had to have Rapunzel's help in order for him to rescue her. It takes more than one to become imprisoned in self-hatred. It takes more than one to become free of self-hatred.

Those who overcome their painful circumstances are set apart from those who become absorbed in self-hatred by these behaviors:

- They choose models that meet their needs in healthy ways. If their parents don't qualify, they select someone else—a teacher, coach, grandparent, etc.
- They enter an intimate relationship with the intention of meeting their partner's needs as well as getting their

needs met. They become aware that making this intention a reality requires that both partners learn to consistently communicate with one another using the interpersonal skills of **E**mpathy (E), **R**espect (R), and **A**uthenticity (A).

The New **ERA** *of Intimacy*

Being able to develop into a healthy individual in a loving relationship is dependent upon your experiencing and modeling healthy relationship behavior. Healing is the dissolving of self-hatred. It gradually comes about as each partner stretches into meeting the other's needs by practicing and becoming increasingly skilled in The ERA Process. Before introducing you to this powerful process in Part III, let's proceed to Part II, where we'll learn much about love and loving.

Make It Known

1.   At an unconscious level you come to believe that you experience pain because you are unworthy of having your needs met. This sense of unworthiness resolves as *self-hatred.*
2.   Everyone has a degree of self-hatred, albeit some more than others.
3.   Self-hatred is the core cause of projection and the core cause of criticism.
4.   *Projection* is when you see another as though s/he is a mirror reflecting a part of yourself. That is, you see in her/him what is really in you.
5.   Every criticism is projection, and every criticism is a form of adaptive behavior, meaning it is born in reactivity.
6.   Those who overcome their painful circumstances are set apart from those who become absorbed in self-hatred by these behaviors:
     a.   They choose models that meet their needs in healthy ways. If their parents don't qualify, they select someone else—a teacher, coach, grandparent, etc.
     b.   They enter an intimate relationship with the intention of meeting their partner's needs as well as getting their needs met. They become aware that making this intention a reality requires that both partners learn to consistently communicate with one another using the interpersonal skills of Empathy, Respect, and Authenticity.
7.   Healing is the dissolving of self-hatred, which gradually occurs as each partner stretches into meeting the other's needs by practicing and becoming increasingly skilled in The ERA Process.

Make It Personal

1. List the major criticisms you have/have had of intimate partners.
2. List the major criticisms that your partner/past partners have had of you.
3. Do you recognize possible projections in the criticisms listed? State rationale.

PART II

Demystifying the Experience of Falling In and Out of Love

Stage One: Romantic Love 4

Finding your Handsome Prince/Beautiful Princess

Where are you hiding, my love?
I have sought you since childhood
When the first rustle of a woman's skirt
And the gentleness of her voice
Filled me with some fierce appetite
For wordless wisdom in the silence of your arms.
I was looking in the subways and the stores
And in the endless motion of the streets,
In proper parties and in the lonely booths
Of dark and quiet bars.

> —James Kavanaugh, *There are Men Too
> Gentle to Live Among Wolves* (1970)

*A*TYPICAL LOVE RELATIONSHIP READS AT THE start like that of the handsome Prince: he happens to be riding through the forest and sees someone attractive and . . .

> Love happens. It is a miracle that happens by grace. We have no control over it; it comes, it lights our lives, and very often it departs. We can never make it happen nor make it stay. (p. 116)
>
> —Irene Claremont deCastillejo,
> *Knowing Woman,*
> *A Feminine Psychology* (1990)

This kind of 70's thinking only served to perpetuate the belief that an out-of-control roller coaster ride of falling in and out of love is inevitable. We now know this is *not true.*

Nonetheless, when love comes, you have found "*The One,*" and everything else pales in significance. Being in love is the elixir of life. Proclaimed through time immemorial in poetry and song lyrics, the ecstasy of newfound love allows no room for insurmountable obstacles. "This time is different!" you assure yourself. You feel omnipotent—nothing can prevent you from claiming your happily ever after.

This experience may happen the first time you meet your intended or it may happen somewhere down the line, but when the fabulous feelings arrive, it's magic. It's as though you have always known him/her. You cannot imagine life without them. Nor can you ever remember feeling so completely satisfied. The presence of these feelings and thoughts is evidence enough— you have found your Handsome Prince/ Beautiful Princess. *You are in love!*

But the coveted experience of *falling in love* is not, from the very start, what it seems to be.

Falling in love feelings are not spontaneous responses to your beloved, despite your belief to the contrary. Because the wonderful feelings arise in his/her presence, you believe the loved one is the source of these feelings. It's time to demystify this experience of *finding "The One"* or *falling in love.* All you'll need to understand this seemingly magical experience is to recognize what's going on within you at an unconscious level.

Everything that you and I experience as meaningful and emotionally significant is permanently encoded in our body. These engrams include the external stimuli that we notice—what we see, hear, touch, taste, and smell—as well as our body's internal response to these stimuli—our thoughts, emotions, sensations, and motor movements. So when a significant aspect of an encoded event is called to mind, other aspects of the event show up along with it.

A few examples will bring this concept to life:

I'll go first: When I see a red-haired dog running toward me, my breathing stops—I freeze. My shoulders hunch as stomach cramps and nausea grab my focus. (A rabid Irish setter bit me in the stomach when I was eight years old and it took seventeen stitches to close the gash.)

Now, it's your turn: Imagine that you are driving down a country road and you smell newly mown grass. A vivid picture of your first hayride flashes in your mind's eye, and you smile at the memory of a stolen kiss.

Or, if you happen to be an Easterner who is big-city bred, picture yourself hustling among the throngs crowding a New York City sidewalk in mid-December. You feel the chill in your bones. Christmas lights twinkle from holiday-decorated windows, and the sounds of horns and sirens are muffled by Christmas carols mingled with the smell of roasting chestnuts. Snowflakes wet your nose. All of a sudden you're a little child again with warm excitement glowing in your chest. Trucking along with your father, your hands have turned warm stuffed into woolen mittens—the left one more so, because it's blanketed in Daddy's giant grasp.

These imaginary examples aren't nearly so impacting as your real-life experiences of this phenomenon. Sometimes these happenings are labeled *déjà vu* and are memorable because they have emotional significance—sometimes pleasant, sometimes terrifying.

Wilder Penfield, a surgeon specializing in focal epilepsy, discovered serendipitously that encoded data can be artificially accessed by placing an electronic probe directly on exposed brain cells. This direct access results in one reliving what is encoded in the stimulated brain cells. Whatever was seen, heard, felt, tasted, or smelled, along with whatever responsive thoughts, emotions, sensations, or motor movements occurred, are *re-experienced*. Fortunately, most of us are not subjected to this kind of unusual experiment.

But what *is* usual in our life is the natural experience of noticing something in a present moment that is similar enough to a past experience that our recognition system perceives a match. The more exact the match, the more completely and vividly the former experience replays—to the extent that it alters our experience of the *present*. This is a form of *regression*, and within the experience, we are unaware that we are reliving the past.

At some point, as differences between present and past experiences become evident, our conscious awareness and discriminating faculties will no longer confuse the present happening with a similar past happening. At that moment, regression ceases. On such occasions, we may or may not daydream for a while about times gone by, but we will *know* that we are daydreaming.

This information becomes relevant and potentially life changing as you consider the impact that these recordings have on your future growth and development, as well as on your relationship potential. And none of your recordings are more significant than those tied to your early caregivers.

Because they were the ones who were meeting your needs, you associated the wonderful feelings you had when your needs were met, with the presence of your caregivers. As a vulnerable infant and later a small child, being able to identify and find the persons who were the source of your sustenance and protection was potentially life saving. You studied these all-powerful beings intently. Every aspect of your caregivers was carefully written in your memory banks. How they smelled—that certain perfume, the odor of tobacco on their breath, the smell of sawdust in their clothes. What they looked like—the turn of their jaw, a crinkle in the forehead when they frowned, the curvature of their hips. How they moved and held their body—perhaps a bouncy gait, stiff neck, or slumped shoulders. And what they sounded like— low resonant tones, their footsteps on the stairs, a Southern drawl.

The good feelings—excitement, extraordinarily sharpened senses, anticipation of pleasure, high energy, contentment, safety—that welled up in response to having your childhood needs met, are fixed in your body's memory too. And they are riveted to the recorded images of the caregivers who met those needs.

For instance, whenever I see my aunt, now that she has grown older, I feel cozy, warm, secure, content—just like I felt years ago, back in the cot on granny's screened-in porch—all tucked in with a gently worn, fluffy comforter, listening to the coos of the mourning doves. My aunt's robust laugh, soft rounded body, and snow-white curls that she ties back with a narrow satin ribbon, remind me of my granny.

The composite of all of these images and experiences are encoded in our subconscious. Included in these engrams are all of our feeling responses to the experiences. While various theorists have named this inner record ("Imago" and "Love Map" are examples), we will call it our Intimate Partner Profile (IPP).

When you begin looking for love, your radar scans in search of that special someone who is "interesting," who "turns you on." And you know you have found *"The One"* when you experience fabulous feelings in their presence—excitement, anticipation of pleasure, high energy, contentment, safety. All your senses seem extraordinarily sharpened.

Do these feelings sound familiar? They are exactly the same as those mentioned when your childhood needs were met by your caregivers. Each of us has our own unique set of feelings but whatever they were with your caregivers, they will be identical in the presence of your new love.

These fabulous feelings replay because the beloved is a close enough match to your *Intimate Partner Profile*—all the images of your caregivers that are stored in your memory banks—that the feelings you had as a child in the presence of those caregivers, surface again in the presence of the beloved. That is, when the stored image is activated, the stored internal response locked to that image is also activated. A person who triggers this experience in you, is called an *"Intimate Partner Profile Match" or "IPP Match."* In those moments when you think you are experiencing new *falling in love* feelings, you are actually re-experiencing feelings from your past. The impact that these past feelings have on your present and future is almost beyond belief.

The activation of this particular historic happening is a very special event. Given that you were younger back then, you had experienced less life trauma, and were more energetic and vital—literally more fully alive than you became later. Plus, you were excited with the expectation and experience of having your needs met by the omnipotent caregivers. So, now that you are a more traumatized, less vital adult, the reawakened state of childhood feels especially grand.

As an adult, you are unaware of the source of these grand feelings; you don't realize that you're experiencing a replay of an historic event. You think you are *in love*. The intensity of your feelings depends on the closeness of the Intimate Partner Profile Match. The more similarities between your beloved and your early caregivers, the more intense the replay of feelings; that is, the more *in love* you are. This regressed state is called *Romantic Love*, and is the first stage of a primary intimate relationship.

While you're remembering times gone by, take a moment to reminisce about your introduction to romance. What drifts into your memory from that unforgettable once-in-a-lifetime experience?

I don't even have to close my eyes to go back to those magical moments:

It was a blind date—at least for me. He lived and went to school in a little town nearby, but he had seen me walking out of the movie theatre and had somehow gotten my name and phone number. After checking around, I agreed he could come to my house Sunday afternoon after church.

From the minute I opened the door and laid eyes on him, I was enchanted. Standing there was the best-looking guy I had ever seen. Curly blond hair crowned a six-foot-tall, broad-shouldered athlete. His mouth curved into a smile and, looking down at me, he said, "Hi, I'm Jerry."

That afternoon I sat in the front porch swing with the most charming guy imaginable, just talking. I don't remember what we talked about. It doesn't matter. But after all these years, my heart still races just thinking about those times.

Six weeks later, Jerry gave me his letter jacket to wear, proof that we were "going steady." How I loved wearing that jacket! It held his fragrance, keeping him with me all the time, and I felt so secure—and super proud. It hung almost to the bottom of my skirt and I had to fix the pushed up sleeves with rubber bands, but I didn't care—it reminded me of how big and strong he was.

Jerry was my first experience with romantic passion, and during those long talks on the porch with only the streetlight to break the darkness, we hatched our secret plan. As soon as I graduated, we would marry.

I wore his letter jacket for two years.

The summer following his high school graduation, Jerry was drafted. I entered the eleventh grade as he shipped off to Germany, where he would spend his two-year hitch. We'd get out within months of one another. The timing was perfect.

For a while, writing and receiving love letters stuffed with pictures of Jerry in his uniform was exciting, and the varied poses in front of foreign backgrounds fueled my fantasies and filled my need for intimate companionship. But I got tired of missing him and being lonely, and soon I was mainly just bored. Less than three months later, though guilt-ridden, I sent him a "Dear John" letter. At sixteen, I was not prepared to be "engaged" while all my friends were having fun dating.

When he showed up at my freshman dorm two years later, handsome as ever, the magic was gone. We were strangers. There had simply been too much growing apart. But Jerry will always live in that special place hearts reserve for the first real love.

Hopefully, my recollections have stimulated a pouring forth of your heart's memories. Regardless, these recordings of our first experiences of being in love—whether or not we consciously remember them—have altered us indelibly, and have influenced the relationship choices we have made ever since.

Because falling in love and being in love are actually replays of historic feelings, you will predictably fall out of love when you stop perceiving your partner as an *Intimate Partner Profile Match*. And the match will inevitably begin to crumble soon after you've committed to being together—whether the commitment includes marriage or not.

The presence and strength of these historic replays are greatly affected by the amount of contact that you have with your beloved. If you don't have *enough* contact to keep the *Intimate Partner Profile* (IPP) activated, the treasured feelings cease. Perhaps the old saying "Absence makes the heart grow fonder" would be more accurate with the addition "of somebody else."

In order to keep the Intimate Partner Profile alive, we're compulsive about staying in touch with our love. One way is to keep something that reminds us of him/her—like a picture, a gift, or something that belongs to him/her (like Jerry's letter jacket that I wore constantly). Listening to "our song," revisiting favorite spots, or listening to her/his voice on their answering machine are other ways of keeping the image fresh. If the projection fades, the feelings go away. And the stark contrast of not having the good feelings versus having them is so painful—particularly if you're afraid s/he won't return—that you may feel as if you're going to die.

Incidentally, if you are unfortunate enough for your beloved to go out of your life before the projection breaks down, you can be forever stuck with the illusion that the perfect partner got away. You may know someone who mourned the loss of an unrequited love for a lifetime. What a waste! Let's not count ourselves among these unhappy souls. Had the-one-that-got-away just stuck around long enough, they too would have fallen from favor.

Just as *not enough* contact results in the vibrant feelings going away, *too much* contact also results in their demise. Now "Absence makes the heart grow fonder" seems to fit. Your contact must be limited for the same reason that you need contact in the first place: because your internal responses are locked to the historic image. Your projection must be upheld. In other words, your beloved must look and behave enough like your *Intimate Partner Profile* for you to stay deluded, and therefore regressed.

And the more you are around her/him, the more you are bombarded with ways in which s/he does not live up to the idealized image that you have projected onto them. You notice that s/he does things that you never thought they would do; and s/he doesn't do things you anticipated that they, as the perfect partner, would do. S/he becomes someone you have never known.

The disillusionment of "You're not who I thought you were" turns into frustration and anger. You may charge your partner with deceiving you: "You've changed! You're not the person I fell in love with!" The in-love feelings disappear. This makes total sense, given that "I love you" during the Romantic Stage really means "Aha! I think you can meet my needs."

As the awareness dawns that your partner is not who you thought s/he was, romantic love dies. You begin to see your partner as a no-longer-so-attractive stranger who is not meeting your needs. It's no wonder that the new message becomes "I'm not in love with you anymore"—one of the most dreaded utterances in the English language.

The truth is, you haven't loved him/her from the beginning. The relationship that exists in the Romantic Love Stage is the one that each person has with their projected *Intimate Partner Profile* onto their partner. The loving feelings are activated by the projection, not by the partner. When your perception of your partner becomes too dissimilar to your idealized recordings of your early caregivers for you to continue to project those recordings, the in-love feelings disappear.

If your partner's projection of idealized images onto you breaks down first, the roles reverse, and you will be on the receiving end of this drama. Either way, the outcome is painful, and all too often, devastating! Life ceases to hold the promise of happiness and dreams coming true.

Romantic Love has ended. But, then, romantic love always ends in a real (as opposed to a fantasized or projected) relationship. It is a transient stage in the process of self-development, but it is a vital stage.

Vital, first of all, because the in-love feelings allow you to become aware of your potential to feel alive. Second, your internal *Intimate Partner Profile* will attract you to, or have you "pick" a person who will activate the very issues that need resolving for you to reclaim your potential aliveness. And, third, the fabulous feelings are so bonding, they entice you to stay in connection with your partner and try to work through the problems when the pain of the power struggle sets in.

Almost everyone who falls in love (meets an *Intimate Partner Profile* Match) eventually falls out of love. But don't become discouraged with this news—falling out of love is a natural step along your path to Real Love. And Real Love encompasses all the good stuff, including fabulous feelings and passion. But we're getting ahead of ourselves.

That you "pick" someone who will eventually activate your deepest pain is believed by many who are psychologically sophisticated to be a major symptom of maladjustment. Recently, a therapist reluctantly and somewhat shamefully told me that his " 'picker' is broke." He learned that in graduate school. However, it's not possible for a person's " 'picker' to be broke;" your "picker" *is* your "picker."

That you will feel in-love feelings toward someone who will cause you pain in exactly the same ways that your early caregivers caused you pain, is natural. Everybody does. By definition, an *Intimate Partner Profile* Match is someone who has traits similar to those of your early caregivers.

Of course all of us would have fewer wounds had our caregivers been more mature and healthy and had they lived in a more nurturing environment; they could have better met our needs. Clearly they did the best they could, given their own histories. A healthier past would have set us up for a healthier future. Furthermore, were you less wounded and more mature, you would be attracted to a partner who is less wounded and more mature—someone who would be better able to meet your present needs just as you would be better able to meet theirs.

For you can only attract and be attracted to someone who is at your same level of development. Romantic love does not blossom between a relatively well-adjusted person and a relatively maladjusted person. This news may cause you to reflect before you conclude and suggest to others that your partners or ex-partners are/were crazy bums.

Bottom line, you are who you are, and you are dealt the hand you are dealt. And that is the hand you must play. Cursing the dealer or the cards doesn't help you win the game. No manner of finding fault and blaming, or of being envious of another's circumstance, will help; rather such perceptions and behaviors will just keep you stuck so that you never reach happily-ever-after.

If you happen to believe that your "picker" is broke, hopefully, you will be able to discard that mistaken concept. Telling yourself that you *should* be attracted to someone other than the men/women to whom you *are* attracted is folly. You will be drawn to someone who is inclined to behave in ways that are similar to your primary caregivers—both in the ways that saved your life and in the ways that caused you pain and left you wounded. This is just the way it is, and it can be good news or it can be bad news. It all depends on the choices that you make, as you become aware that certain of *your* adaptive behaviors are damaging to your partner.

Your incidents of pain, which are recorded as wounds, must be accessed before they can be healed. Interactions with an Intimate Partner Profile Match will reopen your wounds with uncanny precision. In fact, the more strongly you are romantically attracted to someone, the more adaptive behaviors they will have that are similar to those that caused your initial wounding. It is these very adaptive behaviors, in both you and in your partner, that produce conflict and power struggles. As one partner becomes emotionally expansive, the other partner becomes increasingly withdrawn and unavailable. More and more scabbed-over places are re-injured as each person's reactivity escalates. And these episodes can become inconceivably vicious as the primitive struggle to survive intensifies.

The ancient pain recorded in both you and your partner is reactivated as these wounds are accessed. This "worst-of-times" experience however, *can* be the precursor to a "best-of-times" outcome. While this is as deep a pain as any of us are likely ever to experience, the motivation to remedy it is great. Plus, the reactivity that occurs when your wounds are pricked precisely identifies how you've been wounded, so you can know exactly what you need to be healed. (You remember that if your reactive response is constricting, you need more space; and if your reactive response is expanding, you need more attention.) So, you have incentive and information—not a bad combination!

Make It Known

1. Society teaches that when you feel fabulously alive in a person's presence, you are in love with them. Therefore, when you cease to experience the fabulous feelings in his/her presence, you are no longer in love with them. In other words, you have fallen in love when the feelings begin, and you have fallen out of love when they end. This interpretation of the presence of these feelings within you is inaccurate.

2. Everything that you and I experience that is meaningful and emotionally significant is permanently encoded in our body. These engrams include external stimuli that you notice along with the internal responses you had to those stimuli. The body's response is riveted to the event that stimulated it. This means that if you experience either the internal bodily response or the external event, the other is simultaneously activated.

3. When you notice something in the present that happens to be similar enough to something that you noticed in the past, your recognition system perceives a match. This activates the images from the past along with the internal feeling responses that accompanied them. That is, you literally experience a replay of these past encodings as an overlay of your present experiencing. (An analogy might be a recording event when an artist dubs one soundtrack on top of another. The difference is that all the senses are involved in your replay, not just audio.) This phenomenon occurs outside of your conscious awareness. You don't know that what you're experiencing is partially in the present and partially a replay from the past (regression).

4. The term *Intimate Partner Profile* is used to designate the composite of all the images and experiences of your early caregivers which have been encoded in your body. Included in these engrams are all of the feeling responses that you had toward your caregivers—some of which were fabulous feelings that you experienced as a young child.

5. An *Intimate Partner Profile* Match is someone whom you perceive at an unconscious level to be your early caregiver/s. This is because they have sufficient characteristics similar to those recorded in your *Intimate Partner Profile*. This unconscious recognition activates the historic fabulous feelings that are riveted to the caregiver images in your body's memory banks.

6. Having these fabulous aliveness feelings in the presence of an "other" is experienced as falling in love. Actually, it is a projection based on a regressive experience. This phenomenon is the first stage of a love relationship and is called the Romantic Love Stage.

7. So long as falling in love and being in love are equated with experiencing the historic feelings that come up in the presence of an *Intimate Partner Profile* Match, you will predictably fall out of love (cease experiencing the replay of the positive historic feelings) whenever you stop perceiving the other person as an idealized *Intimate Partner Profile* Match.

8. The relationship that exists in romantic love is the relationship that you have with your idealized *Intimate Partner Profile* projected onto your partner. The in-love feelings are activated by your projections; not by your partner. When your perception of your partner becomes too dissimilar to the positive recordings of early caregivers

for you to continue to project those images, the in-love feelings disappear.

9.   Romantic love always *ends* in real—as opposed to fantasized or projected—relationships. It is a transient stage in the process of self-development that is essential in learning how to create real, lasting love relationships.

10.   Romantic love serves three vital functions in individual growth and development and in the potential for your wounds to be healed:

   a. The in-love feelings that consciously replay so wonderfully when you experience an Intimate Partner Profile Match allows you to become aware of your potential to feel alive.

   b. Interactions with an Intimate Partner Profile Match identify your wounds by activating your pain and reactivity, pinpointing precisely where and how you need to be healed.

   c. The fabulous feelings are so bonding, they entice you to stay in connection with your partner and work through the problems when the pain of the power struggle sets in.

Make It Personal

1. Write the name of each of your early primary caregivers (the persons who took care of you when you were little) on a separate sheet of paper. Complete the following instructions for each. As best you can, take yourself back to when you were a little child and *write the responses from that little child place in you.*

    a. Make two lists:

        i. List their positive traits/characteristics.

        ii. List their negative traits/characteristics.

    b. Circle in each list under (a) the three traits or characteristics that had the most impact on you when you were young.

    c. Complete the following sentences by filling in the blanks. (Remember to write your responses for *each* of your caregivers from that little-child place in you.)

        i. What you give me that is most valued by me is

            _____.

        ii. What I want/need most from you that I do not get is _____.

        iii. The best times we have together are when

            _____.

        iv. The times with you that are the worst for me are when _____.

    d. Circle the sentences under (c) that have the most impact on you.

2. Again, write the name of each of your early primary caregivers. This time, from the vantage point of *the adult that you are now,* finish sentences (a) and (b) for each of

your caregivers.

   a. The most painful memory I have of you is

      _____.

   b. The most precious memory I have of you is

      _____.

3.   On a separate sheet of paper, entitled "Some Aspects of My Intimate Partner Profile" copy the information that you circled in #1.

4.   Write a paragraph describing what falling in love is like for you. Include:

   a. Whether you tend to be attracted quickly, or over a period of time during which you progress from acquaintance to friend to lover.

   b. What within you tells you that you are falling/have fallen in love.

5.   Write a paragraph describing what falling out of love is like for you.

6.   Write the name of each primary love relationship partner that you have had on a separate sheet of paper. Complete the following instructions in regard to each of the partners. As best you can, answer from the time frame when you were in relationship with him/her.

   a. Make two lists:

      i. List their positive traits/characteristics.

     ii. List their negative traits/characteristics.

   b. Circle in each list under (a) the three traits or characteristics that had the most impact on you when you were in that relationship.

   c. Complete the following sentences by filling in the blanks. (Remember to write your response from the time when you were *in* the relationship.)

    i. What you give me that I most value is

    _____.

    ii. What I want/need from you that I do not get is

    _____.

    iii. The best times we have together are when

    _____.

    iv. The times with you that are the worst for me are
    when _____.

  d. Circle three sentences under (c) that have the most impact on you.

7. Write, once again, the names of all of your primary love relationship partners and finish sentences (a) and (b) for each.

  a. The most painful memory I have of you is

  _____.

  b. The most precious memory I have of you is

  _____.

8. Compare the compiled information about your caregivers that you have recorded on the sheet entitled "Some Aspects of My *Intimate Partner Profile*" with the information about your partners in love relationships. Is a pattern evident? Write down what you notice.

Stage Two: The Power Struggle

5

You're as ugly as I am

Glass shoes break when stepped on
Golden pumpkins drip inside.
Stars lose their glitter at the dawn
With twelve strokes the magic died.

—Alison Southern, 1998.
Unpublished Poem with No Name

E DO NOT GO EASILY INTO THE NIGHT OF FALLING out of love—or more accurately—into the daylight of the present and the real. When the honeymoon is over, giving up the captivating magic of the illusory perfect lover is painful beyond words.

Love-gone-wrong is the favorite theme of country western

songs. No wonder it is the most popular music in America, for most love relationships do "go wrong." We already know that half as many divorces as marriages take place each year in this country. Although we keep trying, second marriages have a greater percentage of divorces than first. And even though statistics vary among studies, it is clear that many who stay married are unhappily married.

To avoid being one of these statistics requires more than self-determination and resolve. In all the years that I have worked with couples experiencing difficulties, I have found very few who started out thinking their union wouldn't last "until death do us part."

But inevitably, difficulties set in and the illusion dissolves. Initially partners notice the withholding of favors and a lack of common courtesies. Blaming and shaming become commonplace, and destructive behaviors escalate—sometimes to the point of violence.

Not all live through their final chapter of abuse. Sadly, far too many of us die prematurely through self-inflicted or "the other"-inflicted mortal wounds. Some survive close calls and with maimed bodies and/or maimed psyches, limp away, divorce papers or not. A percentage of these live with being stalked and/or harassed for years to come. It is no accident that the spouse/ex-spouse is the first suspect when a partner/former partner dies of unnatural causes. Look in any major newspaper any day of the week for the dramatic stories that report these terrible, heartbreaking tragedies.

Yes, the catastrophic exits of suicide and homicide can be added to divorce and breaking up as final exits sometimes taken from "love relationships." Becoming psychotic is another. Ever know anyone who got out of an unbearable love relationship by going crazy?

Truth be known, who among us has not considered one of these desperate acts at some time in the throes of an agonizing conflict with a partner?

The mystery of why a relationship that brings such happiness in the beginning can bring such pain later on, can now be demystified. Just as the first stage, Romantic Love, is a regressive stage dominated by projection, so is the second. However, this time the projections are of the negative characteristics in your *Intimate Partner Profile*. Instead of projecting feelings that you experienced when your childhood needs were met, this time you project the feelings that you experienced when your childhood survival was threatened.

The *Intimate Partner Profile* Match phenomenon, with its replay of grand feelings, causes us to experience those feelings most intensely with the person/s who will eventually activate the greatest pain and growth challenges within us. It plays out like so: when the idealized projections—projections of all of the positive *Intimate Partner Profile* recordings—discontinue, the demonized projections of all of the negative *Intimate Partner Profile* recordings take over. Along with the roses come the thorns.

This is not nature playing a dirty joke on us, though it can certainly feel that way. It's a continuation of the process. Think of it as nature being committed to your healing and completion. The amount of pain that you encounter in the process depends on the amount of pain that you have stored in your body from past experiences (how wounded you are). Pain is created in this process only when you unconsciously replay your historic adaptive behavior.

These latter feelings are replays of stored recordings, just as the in-love feelings were. You react to your needs not being met by your current partner in the same ways that you reacted when your needs weren't met by your early caregivers—as terrified infants, except now you are in an adult body.

As you approach the awareness that "you're not the person I fell in love with," the encroaching prospect of losing the person you thought you had found, seems unbearable. Your body's triggered memory tells you that you can't live without him/her.

You will protest every step along the path of the dissolving idealized Intimate Partner Profile projections. This chaotic and painful period of trying to stay connected with the person who you believe (never mind that your belief is erroneous) is the source of your ability to stay alive is the second stage of intimate relationship and is called the *Power Struggle*. And the higher the ecstasy in the Romantic Love Stage, the deeper the hell in the Power Struggle Stage.

You recall from Chapter 2 that the nature of your reactivity is determined by the nature of the perceived threat. If you perceive that you are being intruded upon—controlled, manipulated, smothered—your body will constrict and you will become rigid, less available, less responsive, closed-minded, emotionally cold, and overly "rational." (Review the *minimizing* phenomenon from pages 36-42.)

On the other hand, if you perceive that you are being neglected—not seen, not heard, not valued—your emotions will escalate and become more intense. You'll feel frustrated, afraid, hurt, and angry, and you will become increasingly "irrational" and more volatile in your attempt to get what you need. (Review the *maximizing* phenomenon from pages 42-50.)

The heartbreaking pain that you experience in your relationships is caused by you and your partner accessing one another's wounds. But your partner's behavior is not the sole cause of your reactivity.

For instance, one of Kay's predictable triggers is her perceiving that a partner feels superior to her. This is not difficult to understand, given Kay's background. At times, she is insecure within herself about her worth and value. What, specifically, is Kay reacting to in those moments that threatens her (causes her pain)?

> Growing up a minister's daughter, Kay and her family were often guests in the homes of parishioners. Sometimes the parishioners' homes were much nicer than Kay's, sometimes not as nice. But Kay and her family were always the guests. As her father pastored increasingly affluent churches, the gap widened. More frequently they were invited into circumstances that were beyond their personal financial means. Kay knew that they were guests in this more privileged world and she perceived that the hosts knew it as well. And she didn't like it.

Particularly when Kay feels inadequate and not-as-good-as, if she perceives that her partner is taking a superior stance, the pain resulting from this perceived slight is piggybacked onto historic pain (her wounds).

> Kay reported a particularly painful episode in our first session. She had recently discontinued a ten-year

relationship. Upon announcing her unwillingness to continue the exclusive relationship given the partner's refusal to propose marriage, he had angrily demanded return of some of the gifts he'd given her. One was a nice watch, which she especially liked. She in turn, had offered to buy it from him. His response to her offer, "You can't afford it," had incurred big-time reactivity.

Forms of the verb "perceive" are used to introduce this example. There may be times during which reactivity is brought on by an accurate perception of your partner. In other instances, you may be projecting the perception, and in still others, you may have provoked the very behavior in them that causes you pain. We tend to draw to ourselves whatever we fear—even if we have to make it up or cause it to happen.

Problems escalate because reactivity, when unchecked, automatically triggers the partner's adaptive behavior. Withdrawing-from elicits intruding-upon behavior, and intruding-upon elicits withdrawing-from behavior. The war is on! And no war results in more personal pain and damage than the one you wage with a partner. The more battles, the more re-wounding.

Although your primary reactive style is the same as when you were a child, the adaptive behavior with which you protest may vary from the child response to behavior that is more "adult." The infant cry, for instance, might be replaced by verbal expressions such as "You hurt my feelings" or "You don't care about anybody but yourself!" Retreating into an activity that excludes your partner, such as overworking or having an affair, are other possible adult derivations. The adaptive behaviors that aren't so different from the ways you behaved as a child include stomping your feet, scowling, screaming, throwing things, slamming doors, and pouting.

Are you able to add to this list, based on what *you* do when you are reactive in an intimate relationship?

When you were little, you learned that these ways worked to get you what you needed, or at least they made life more tolerable by forcing your pain underground when you didn't get what you needed. But these behaviors do not work to get you what you need in an adult relationship. Withdrawing, criticizing, or making demands will not elicit the responses from your partner that you need to be healed and feel loved. In fact, these programmed, automatic responses to pain, your adaptive behaviors, are the most you can do to *prevent* getting your needs met, including your need to feel loved.

And at the same time that your partner is failing to meet your needs, guess what? You are failing to meet his/hers. Remember the wicked witch that we create outside ourselves so long as we are imprisoned by our own self-hatred? As you cease to live up to one another's expectations, the feelings of self-hatred are activated and projected onto each other: "You're as ugly as I am!" It's called *criticism*.

Compulsive criticism is your attempt to force your partner back into being who you *thought* s/he was (your *Intimate Partner Profile* projected onto her/him) when you fell in love. The resulting chaos is a power struggle in which both you and your partner are attempting to stay alive by eliminating one another's uniqueness. That is, by projecting onto or provoking the other, you attempt to make *your* projections *their* reality—so that their true identity goes unnoticed or denied.

Unfortunately, most of us who enter the Power Struggle either literally die while still enmeshed in what is meant to be a transitory phase or we get out of the relationship even less alive than when we entered. In the fifties, Rod McKuen expressed it this way:

> Sometimes I think people were meant to be strangers.
> Not to get to know one another,
> not to get close enough to damage the heart
> made older by each new encounter.
>   —"Channing Way I"
>   *Stanyon Street and Other Sorrows*

Consciously knowing that your criticizing behavior makes you less lovable is not enough to stop the self-defeating behavior. You will be compelled to do it anyway. Your attacks are driven by your survival instinct. No wonder we can be so vicious, given that no matter how much our rational selves know that we are alienating our partner, our more primitive selves learned that if we complain long enough and loud enough, we get the milk.

Primitive survival responses can only be altered by repeatedly selecting to replace them with more mature behavior. Reversing the downward spiral requires that you outgrow your wicked witch (or develop beyond your self-hatred) so that you are capable of meeting your partner's needs and of allowing your partner to meet yours. Only then will the excruciating pain that drives you to hurt and be hurt by one another be eliminated.

In order to become more fully alive, you must discontinue adaptive behavior and stretch into intentional behavior that promotes your growth and development. You will have to reach out in places where you're too restrictive, and relax in places where you're overextended.

Unfortunately, when you first give up your adaptive behaviors of withdrawing, criticizing, and demanding, you are likely to experience the very result that you feared: "I'm doing it, but I'm still not getting what I want." And not only may you not be getting what you want, you may also be getting what you *don't* want, i.e., criticism. It is so difficult to continue to be vulnerable in the beginning, before the payoffs start rolling in. But hang in there a little longer, because you are on a path that will gradually help you grow beyond this stuck place.

Just knowing that the Power Struggle Stage is a natural phase on the journey to mature loving makes it somewhat easier. That you and your partner get sucked into compulsive conflicts is inevitable. The conflicts that make up the Power Struggle are simply growth trying to happen.

Remember, the *IPP Match* phenomenon assures that you fall in love with someone who will trigger all of the painful, unfinished places within you, and that you will trigger all of the painful, unfinished places within them. As difficult as it may be to believe, this is good news. It's natural to be drawn to someone who will access all of your wounds (recordings of out-of-balance pulsing in your body), so that the wounds can be healed (balance can be restored).

This personal story may help you understand the potential benefit of going through the Power Struggle:

One evening my younger son Chris, who was fourteen at the time, complained of a terrible side ache. When I poked in the location of his appendix, he yelped, nearly jumping out of his skin. I immediately loaded him into the car and rushed to the hospital emergency room. With parental adrenaline in overdrive, I announced that Chris had appendicitis and needed attention STAT. The nurse in charge reacted to my diagnosis with a "Just-where-did-you-get-your-medical-license-from?" look in her eyes, but she contacted the surgeon on call anyway.

Emergency surgery began within thirty minutes that same night. The next morning, the surgeon who had performed the operation told me that had we waited a few hours more, Chris's appendix would have burst. So even though his pain was great when I poked where he was damaged, the alternative pain would have been far worse. Furthermore, he could have died.

Knowing where the pain is, is important. It brings you directly to the place where healing needs to happen. And healing is what occurs within your partner when you stretch into consistently giving them what they've needed for so long.

Perhaps the words of Jerry M. Lewis, M.D., an eminent marital and family researcher, will provide the incentive for you to take the next step:

For those who do not construct a healing relationship, there is a strong likelihood that the painful past will be relived, often over and over again. And this underscores the necessity to think deeply about the central relationship patterns in life. (The Preface)

—Disarming the Past (1999)

Make It Known

1. The Power Struggle, like Romantic Love, is a regressive stage dominated by projection. However, in the Power Struggle, the projections are of the negative characteristics in your *Intimate Partner Profile*, the feelings that you experienced when your childhood survival was threatened. You react to your needs not being met by your current partner in the same ways that you reacted when your needs were not met by your early caregivers.

2. As you approach the awareness that "you're not the person I fell in love with," the encroaching prospect of losing the person you thought you had found seems unbearable. Your body's triggered memory tells you that you can't live without him/her. This chaotic and painful period of trying to stay connected with the person who you believe (never mind that your belief is erroneous) is the source of your ability to stay alive, is the second stage of intimate relationship and is called the *Power Struggle*.

3. The nature of your reactivity is determined by the nature of the perceived threat. If you feel intruded upon, you will constrict; if you feel neglected, your emotions will escalate and become more intense.

4. Sometimes reactivity is brought on by an accurate perception of your partner. In other instances, you may be projecting the perception, and in still others, you may have provoked the very behavior in them that causes you pain. We tend to draw to ourselves whatever we fear, even if we have to make it up or cause it to happen.

5. The heartbreaking pain that you experience in your

relationships is partially caused by you and your partner accessing one another's wounds. But your partner's behavior is not the sole cause of your reactivity.

6. As partners cease to live up to each other's expectations, their feelings of self-hatred are activated and projected onto one another.

7. Compulsive criticism is an attempt to force your partner back into being who you thought s/he was (your Intimate Partner Profile projected onto her/him) when you fell in love with them. The resulting chaos is a power struggle in which both partners are attempting to stay alive by eliminating the other's uniqueness.

8. You must outgrow your wicked witch (develop beyond your self-hatred) in order to be capable of meeting your partner's needs and allowing your partner to meet yours. Only then will the excruciating pain that drives you to hurt and be hurt by one another be eliminated.

9. To become more fully alive, you must discontinue adaptive behavior and stretch into intentional behavior that promotes growth and development.

10. The conflicts that make up the Power Struggle are simply growth trying to happen.

11. The *Intimate Partner Profile* Match phenomenon assures that you fall in love with someone who will trigger all of the painful, unfinished places within you, and that you will trigger all of the painful, unfinished places in him/her.

12. Knowing where the pain is, is important. It brings you directly to the place where healing needs to happen. And healing is what occurs when you and your partner consistently stretch into meeting one another's needs.

Make It Personal

1. Make a list of the major complaints that you have/have had of love relationship partners. (Be sure to include what they *do* and what they *don't do* that is most frustrating for you.)
2. What form does your reactivity typically take in response to these frustrating experiences—*minimizing* or *maximizing*? How do you feel when you are reactive? What adaptive behaviors do you employ?
3. Make a list of the major complaints that your partners have of you. Record themes or patterns you notice.
4. What form does your partner's reactivity typically take in response to these frustrating experiences—*minimizing* or *maximizing*? Has s/he told you how they feel during these times? Write what you perceive her/his feelings are when they are reactive. (You may want to ask your partner if your perceptions are accurate.)
5. What adaptive behaviors does your partner employ?
6. How do you respond to your partner's adaptive behaviors?
7. Can you imagine that both you and a partner must learn to do something other than withdrawing, criticizing, and making demands of one another, if you are ever to move beyond the Power Struggle into a mature, loving relationship?

PART III

Learning How to Create a Real and Lasting Love Relationship

Stage Three: Awareness 6

Letting your hair down and opening up your heart

The minute I heard my first love story,
I started looking for you.
Not knowing how blind that was.
Lovers don't finally meet somewhere
They're in each other, all along.

—Rumi

BEFORE SHE SAW THE HANDSOME PRINCE AND he saw her through the castle tower window, Rapunzel had spent years imprisoned in the turret that had no door. *Seeing one another* is the essential first step toward two people potentially creating a loving relationship.

117

We can see another from afar and we can see another up close. Seeing from afar can be a random happenstance. Rapunzel was just looking out the tower window. The Handsome Prince was just riding through the forest. But seeing one another up close does not happen serendipitously. Both people must be intentional in making it happen.

Even handsome princes and fair maidens in fairy tales can make connection only with one another's help. The Prince told Rapunzel what he needed to reach her: for her to let her hair down. This request was not an attempt on the Prince's part to manipulate or control Rapunzel, rather he was openly revealing his truth: He could not, without her cooperation, rescue her. He needed her help to make the connection happen. Specifically, he needed her to provide access to her prison, the key to her heart.

Although in the Romantic Stage an Intimate Partner Profile Match seemingly steals our heart away, real love becomes possible only as each partner freely chooses to *give* the other the key to his/her heart. The key is *what we need to feel loved*. And only as you discover what your needs are, and reveal them in a way that your partner can know them, does the possibility exist that your needs will ever be met. And vice versa. If each partner decides to use the other's *key* by gifting them accordingly, each can become healed and whole, and together they can create an intimate, mature love relationship.

Creating a happily-ever-after requires sufficient information, time, effort, and commitment to do the work. Doing the work means: (1) discovering the key to one another's heart, and (2) learning the process of how to work with others' keys so that both hearts open to healing and to growing.

You've learned that most people's experience in love relationships has been confined to two stages: Romantic Love and the Power Struggle. You've also learned that most of your behavior within these stages has been influenced primarily by your psychological history. In your attempt to have a relationship, you have been doing what comes naturally based upon your thinking patterns and your feelings—and it has gotten you what it has gotten you.

Continuing in the same patterns will continue to get you the same historic results. The more times you repeat the pattern, the more difficult it will be for you to break out of the well-worn ruts. On the other hand, the more evident the ruts will become.

To say that moving beyond the Power Struggle is not easy is a colossal understatement. You experience the first two stages of intimate relationships automatically because they're natural stages—natural in that they're driven by your past.

The three potential stages of intimate relating, Awareness, Transformation and Real Love, do not occur automatically. They become possible only as you develop both by learning specific kinds of information about yourself, about your partner, and about loving relationships, and by consciously and intentionally applying this information as you learn valuable interpersonal relationship skills.

The process of discovering where your and your partner's wounds are, and learning what behaviors will be required for each of you to heal and grow, is called *Awareness*—the third stage of a primary intimate relationship.

Unfortunately, you have been programmed to believe the fable that loving or being in love is the surging of fabulous feelings. Though it may seem contradictory, the probability of learning otherwise increases as you become more disillusioned and hopeless in your unenlightened quest for happily-ever-after. It is as though we have to hit the proverbial bottom—that sinking, black pit of despair—before we're willing to open our mind and heart to ideas and behaviors beyond those we've learned through life experience. Facing the reality that what you've learned has brought you to a dead and unfulfilled end, can beckon the humility of spirit you need to risk opening your mind to possibilities that have been unthinkable before this time.

To even consider that the very qualities that you find unacceptable in your partner really live, denied and disowned, within yourself is a quantum leap in consciousness. But this is the path that your thinking must embrace. To grow beyond self-hatred, or to state it positively, to grow into loving yourself, you must be willing to probe within, discover your deepest wounds, and acknowledge the destructive effects of your adaptive behavior.

The next step is choosing to forsake your adaptive behaviors, the very behaviors that life has taught you are life preserving. Taking this step will go against your every grain. It will feel as though you're exposing yourself to the most treacherous of circumstances without armor and without weapons. You can't believe that you will survive this vulnerable undertaking, for belief comes only from experience. Rather, you will feel as though taking this risk will be your final step toward obliteration and/or permanent isolation.

Sadly, for some, this step is too terrifying, and they give up on the quest for Real Love. Two incidents come to mind where this is exactly what happened—one exited by divorce, the other by murder:

The first happened a number of years back. A woman had been trying for some time to persuade her husband to enter couples therapy to work on their marriage. Finally he agreed to attend a session.

As they file into my office, I sense her hopeful anticipation. We are sitting down and I am about to welcome them when . . . "I'm here for only one reason today," the pillar-of-the-community husband announces, "and I might as well not waste time."

His wife's body goes rigid, and her face pales as his words continue. "For some time now I've been trying to tell her (not missing a beat while he motions in his wife's direction while continuing to look directly at me) that if a marriage between two people is right, it works. If they can't get along without having to work at it, then it wasn't meant to be. Our marriage has been over for years, and it's time to end the farce."

Facing and addressing his wife for the first time since entering the office, he continues, "I've already leased an apartment and I'm moving out this weekend. I'd like us both to use Larry [their family lawyer]. Of course, you know I'll do the right thing."

Looking toward the door, he concludes, "Now, if you ladies will excuse me, I have an important meeting to attend."

Having delivered his speech, he stands, almost imperceptibly touches his snow-white cuffs as if to assure that they're still perfectly extended beyond his coat sleeves, and strides out of the room.

The second incident took place more recently.

I was glancing over the *Fort Worth Star Telegram* when the

headline of a front-page article caught my eye: *Wife Says She Shot Husband During Attack*. The shooting had occurred the night before she was allegedly to move into a shelter for battered women.

> . . . She fell apart when she was informed that he was dead. . . . The two had lived together for just over a year and had married in the spring. She loved him very much. . . . At first he wanted to be a very good husband, but when it turned out not to be a fairy tale . . . it was . . . more than he bargained for. . . . (November 20, 1998)

These desperate individuals couldn't see any alternative to their plight other than to end it. Fortunately, you're learning that relationships don't have to reach a dead end, even though there will be times when your pain will be triggered so strongly, that you won't feel able to stop your adaptive behavior from replaying.

If, in spite of your fears and seeming inability to carry through, you shore yourself up and summon the courage to step into vulnerability, it will be the most potentially healing and growth-producing step that you will ever take.

Discovering the Key to Your Heart

When you have a medical problem and go to a physician, the first order of business is for her/him to determine the nature of your illness or injury—s/he makes a diagnosis. This is essential to her/his prescribing the treatment that will bring you back to health.

So it is with your psychological wounds—the first step is to determine their nature (make the diagnosis). Identifying where you are wounded positions you to determine precisely what you need that you did not historically receive. Only then can the prescription for your healing, the key to your heart, be crafted.

And though the prescription is vital, it is not enough for healing to take place. The prescription must be followed! That is, this information must be communicated clearly and respectfully to your partner, who, by overcoming his/her inclination to respond in ways similar to your early caregivers that were hurtful, must stretch into providing what you have communicated you need. Only then can your deepest wounds be healed. And vice versa. You must stretch into doing the same for her/him. Each of you mature as you intentionally behave in ways that meet the other's needs.

To reinforce these concepts about interpersonal growth and healing, recall that a wound is an encoding of pain that you experienced in the past because a need was not met. Healing happens when that need *is* met. It is your responsibility to tell your partner exactly what the needed behavior is, so that s/he can stretch into giving it to you. This allows you to feel loved and lovable in the parts of yourself previously alienated, thereby releasing your self-hatred.

And vice versa. You must be willing to stretch into doing the same for your partner. The process is possible only when both do it. Healing and being healed is not a spectator sport; this sport requires two active and involved players.

(Incidentally, for those of you who are not currently with a partner, but who would like to begin the healing process so that your next relationship will have a better chance, read on. Specific guidelines follow in the next section.)

There is no hierarchy between partners in a true love relationship; love mates are equals. Not necessarily equal in some of the ways in which the world might measure equality, such as level of formal education, monetary assets, or physical beauty. But equal in one another's eyes—of equal worth, having equal weight in decision-making, deserving of equal respect. Mature, loving partners are committed to the total welfare of each other.

Remarkably, as you discover the specific nurturing behaviors that you require to be healed, or to feel loved, you'll have identified the very behaviors that your partner needs to develop within his/her self to become a more mature and whole person. And your partner's healing will require from you the behaviors that you need to develop within your self so that you can be more mature and whole.

However, when either of you acts according to your adaptive behavioral inclinations, you will surely re-wound each other. You must lay down your swords and take off your bulletproof vests if you are ever to be available to experience intimacy. In other words: Becoming vulnerable is a prerequisite to becoming intimate.

Asking for what you need, and being available to receive it if your partner chooses to give it to you, feels terribly risky, just as it feels risky to open yourself to giving what your partner asks.

When Rapunzel gave the Handsome Prince what he asked by letting her hair down, she was using the key to his heart. Simultaneously, by honoring his request, she enabled him to meet her need to be freed from her prison. It takes two people in cooperative effort to open each other's heart. Each provides the key to their own dark places, and the other turns the key in the lock and gently lets the light illuminate the darkness.

The following example from my personal history illustrates how the keys to our hearts can be used for healing:

Terry, a man I had been in an exclusive relationship with for several years, and I were going to a dinner-dance. I was excited. Ballroom dancing is my favorite pastime and, because I had been on the road working, we hadn't been dancing in weeks.

After settling in as one of three couples around the formally bedecked table, I noticed that everyone was laughing and entering into the festive spirit of the evening. That is, everyone except Terry. In a somewhat joking manner, I said, "Well, you could at least *look* like you're having a good time." His body visibly stiffened and his face turned to stone.

I was angry immediately. I had seen that response before. I knew the fun I had been so looking forward to was *not* going to happen. He would sulk the rest of the evening. So I sarcastically said (mind you, dinner had not even been served and the band leader was just introducing the first rumba), "Are you ready to leave?"

"Yes," he answered firmly.

That was it! We got up, didn't bother with the social niceties of excusing ourselves from the table, and stalked out. Less than half an hour from when we had entered the parking garage engaged in spontaneous conversation, we drove out, sullen and silent.

Ten or fifteen minutes into the drive home (it seemed like an eternity), I was alternating between feeling sorry for myself and being furious with Terry. Tentatively, I thought, "Okay. I know from what I'm learning about reactivity that what I said must have been hurtful or he wouldn't have gone rigid."

A burst of anger and a blurted internal rebuttal: "So

what! He knew I really wanted to have a good time and he didn't care!"

Once again, I was struggling. "Stop my automatic thoughts," I told myself. "I've got to demonstrate that I care about his feelings, and I mustn't sound angry."

I took several deep breaths and then said, with as much sincerity and concern as I could muster, "What I said to you must have been really hurtful."

Silence.

Just as I was about to revert to being angry again, he spoke.

His voice was soft and sad, nostalgic: "I get so tired of people telling me to smile.

"When I was about seven or eight, I was playing baseball with a bunch of kids up the street when a baseball whammed me in the mouth. Broke off my two front teeth." Deep audible breath. "They looked *really* bad, kind of jagged-like." He paused as he rubbed those upper teeth with the inside of his cupped right forefinger. "We couldn't afford to get them fixed right away and the other kids made fun of me." Another deep, audible breath. "I learned to keep my mouth closed. Guess it's been hard to smile ever since."

No more anger. It was gone. I felt such compassion for the little boy who was made fun of when he smiled with those jagged teeth. I couldn't believe Terry hadn't told me this story before.

All those years of my needing him to smile when we were together might have played out very differently if only I had known.

Looking back on this relationship, the dynamics make sense. Terry used to say that my smiling all the time was the thing that first attracted him. Come to think of it, in the beginning, I thought his unsmiling face was mysterious and provocative.

In many obvious ways he reminded me of my daddy. Head-turning handsome, slender, black hair and dark skin, he looked like him. And he was gentle, kind, sensitive, intelligent, multi-talented—a Renaissance man—also like my father.

And then there were ways that were not so obvious; at least not at the time. I now realize that Daddy suffered periodically from depression. Although he put on a "good front" by smiling when he was around people, his eyes almost always looked sad. Daddy's most frequent and most memorable admonition to me from as far back as I can remember, until he died, was "Be a sweet girl!" It was his substitute for "Goodbye." (Weird that Terry said this exact sentence in exactly the same manner to me.)

I obviously interpreted Daddy's admonition, perhaps largely because of his modeling, to mean "Put on a happy face, no matter how you feel." Even when I wasn't happy, I couldn't let it show. So I felt that if I didn't "Be a sweet girl" by looking pleasant and happy all the time, I'd be unacceptable, and people wouldn't want to be around me. I had reacted to my fear of being abandoned by *maximizing*. Specifically, I had learned to model my father's adaptive behavior—smiling and pretending to be happy, regardless of my true feelings.

Terry, on the other hand, had been shamed (which is a form of intrusion) so he had reacted by *minimizing*. Specifically, he had learned to be non-expressive, which to me looked like frowning. Although he didn't let negative feelings show either, I mainly noticed that happy feelings were not expressed. Most of the time, he seemed depressed. Even when he would occasionally *say* he was happy, his face almost never *looked* happy.

Terry's dour expression had held him back in his even being able to *feel* happy feelings. He needed to develop smiling behavior again so that he could reclaim his capacity to feel as well as to show happy feelings, thereby becoming more authentic, thus more whole.

As our relationship progressed through time, Terry began to get upset with me when I smiled, he said, at other men. He also sometimes thought I was making fun of him when I was trying to act happy to cheer both of us up.

So at least part of what Terry needed from me was for me to be more discriminating in my smiling behavior, so that his wounding by being shamed could be healed.

And I clearly needed Terry to alter his adaptive behavior of maintaining a non-expressive face. I needed him to be authentic with his facial expressions, which included his smiling and exuding happiness when he was actually feeling happy. That would have helped me be more authentic with my facial expressions, including feeling free not to smile when I didn't feel like it.

Terry's need for me to alter my adaptive behavior of smiling all the time is something that I had needed to do so that my wounding from fearing abandonment could be healed. My fake smile had communicated that I was phony and had held me back in interpersonal relationships and in my own personal growth. And as I learned to be more authentic, I felt more grounded.

Terry and I, as with all Intimate Partner Profile-matched couples, were wounded in exactly the same area. We had each learned that showing certain feelings with nonverbal facial expressions wasn't acceptable, and we had adapted by discontinuing the unacceptable behaviors. Predictably, we had been wounded from opposite wounding patterns.

Terry no longer has jagged teeth. People no longer make fun of him when he smiles. In fact, he has a beautiful smile. I no longer have a depressed daddy who is smiling and telling me to "Be a sweet girl." In fact, some people have told me they really like my authentic responses.

Adaptive behavior will keep you stuck in the past. You must learn to let go of your adaptive behavior and stretch into meeting your partner's needs, for the behaviors that s/he needs from you is the exact prescription of what you need to develop within yourself if you are to grow up and become mature.

Of course, I was much more aware of *my* needs than I was aware of Terry's. This is usual, especially regarding issues where we've reached an impasse. Our own world makes perfect sense; our partner's world rarely does. True empathy is hard to come by.

No attempt that we make in life will require more courage, perseverance, and willingness to risk as knowing and being known by another. Nonetheless, the potential that exists in the structure of a love relationship for individuals to be healed and to become whole is awesome!

You are probably already aware, at least to some degree, of where your sensitive places are—the words or actions that tend to pierce your heart (cause you to become reactive). But in order for your partner to help you heal, s/he needs specific information. And for you to be able to give it to her/him, you must be very clear as to what your unfulfilled needs are (what causes you pain).

The following exercise will help you discover, step by step, the key to your heart.

Finding the Key to Your Heart

STEP I

The number one instruction under "Make It Personal" at the end of Chapter 5 is to "Make a list of the major complaints that you have of love relationship partners." If you've not yet made that list, *do it now.*

> Example: Major complaints that I have of partners with whom I have or have had a love relationship:
>
> 1. He's late for appointments.
> 2. He spends money he doesn't have (e.g., uses credit cards).
> 3. He thinks he's always right.

STEP II

Before going further, review the information on pages 25-27 regarding reactivity and adaptive behavior.

STEP III

Essentially, the list that you composed in Step I is a list of some of your partner's and/or former partner's adaptive behaviors. Take your list, and one by one, place each item from that list in the following sentence and complete it by filling in the blanks:

"When (<u>my partner</u>) (<u>item from my list</u>), I (<u>minimize or maximize</u>). When I'm being reactive, I feel (<u>state the feeling/s</u>) which I express by (<u>my adaptive behavior</u>)."

You will notice that your reactivity, which you experience as a feeling, is stronger in response to some triggers than to others. The stronger your reactivity, the more desperately you need something other than what you're getting in that circumstance.

First Example: When <u>John is late for an appointment</u> , I <u>maximize</u> . When I'm being reactive, I feel <u>diminished, unimportant, and angry</u> which I express by <u>berating, lecturing, and criticizing him</u> .

Second Example: When <u>Rochelle is late for an appointment</u> , I <u>minimize</u> . When I'm being reactive, I feel <u>disinterested</u> (notice that this is not really a feeling), which I express by <u>ignoring her, being preoccupied, and paying special attention to other people</u> .

STEP IV

Once again, take the list that you wrote for Step I and rewrite each of the sentences on another piece of paper, changing the format as follows:

"When (<u>my partner</u>) (<u>item from your list</u>), the part that bothers/bothered me most is (<u>fill-in-the-blank</u>). I can imagine that this part bothers me most because it reminds me of a way that I experienced being treated during my childhood that was hurtful to me."

It's not necessary at this time for you to recall a happening from your childhood that validates the written statement. Memories will gradually return as you do this work.

Example: "When John is <u>late for an appointment</u> , the part that bothers me most <u>is that he never acknowledges that he's left me waiting, nor does he apologize</u> . I can imagine that this part bothers me most because it reminds me of a way that I experienced being treated during my childhood that was hurtful to me."

Each complaint or frustration that you listed in Step I has, beneath it, an unfulfilled desire. And this unfulfilled desire has gone unmet for a very long time. That you have these desires is not bad or neurotic or sinful or immature. Wanting to be whole and fully alive is completely natural, healthy, and in keeping with your human nature.

STEP V

Take the items from your original list made in Step I and translate each frustration into the unfulfilled desire behind it.

"My unfulfilled desire behind (<u>a complaint from your list</u>) is (<u>unfulfilled desire</u>)."

Example: My unfilled desire behind <u>your being late for an appointment is to feel valued and respected by you</u> .

You are giving invaluable information here! Telling your partner your desires is exactly what s/he needs to know to be able to open your heart. The composite of your unfulfilled desires is the key to your heart. *This is how you give up criticisms: you replace it with saying what you desire.*

But, and this is a big "but," you will never consistently have your desires met by withdrawing from or by intruding upon your partner, which is what all of us do when we're hurt and aren't being conscious and intentional. The partner whose major style is minimizing tends to focus on what s/he *doesn't* want and *is* getting, whereas the partner whose major style is maximizing is likely to focus more on what s/he *does* want and *isn't* getting. Transferring your intentional focus *from* what you don't want and aren't receiving, *to* what you do want and can receive, makes it possible for you to love and be loved.

So, once again, what is the key to your heart? Simple. It is having the desires behind your unmet childhood needs, met. This is what you need to feel loved. Only you know the combination; only you can provide it.

And the key to your partner's heart? The same. Whatever s/he needs to feel loved. Developing a mature, fulfilling relationship, in which you both obtain the elusive goal of loving and being loved, requires that each of you look inward, acknowledge your own needs, and in vulnerability, make them clearly known to the other.

How to Work with Keys
So that Both Hearts Open
to Healing and Growing

Once you identify what you need to feel loved, the next step is to communicate to your partner the *specific behaviors* that would fill those desires and/or meet those needs. In other words, once the key is crafted, you must give it to your partner, along with clear instructions as to how to use it to open your heart.

The key to your heart is a gift not easily given. For allowing another to know what will open your heart means that s/he will have the power to do just that. When s/he uses your key, you will be open to loving and being loved, but you will also be open to re-wounding. It can happen. It probably has happened to you before. Open isn't discriminating. Open is alive and exposed, vulnerable not only to whatever the present may bring, but also to the historic pain that is stored in your body (your old wounds).

However, you must take this risk of opening your heart if your stored pain is *ever* to be healed. Guarantees do not come with being alive. Risking being vulnerable is the only game in town if you truly desire an intimate, loving relationship.

At the same time, opening yourself to give or to receive in intimacy is a choice that is worthy of as much wisdom as you can generate. Determining when and with whom to share your key deserves your very best discriminating ability. And developing your capacity to distinguish between healthy stretching and unhealthy self-sacrifice is essential.

Recall that when the concept of stretching was introduced (the example of Sam in the beginning of Chapter 2), it was defined as the process of reclaiming discontinued behaviors that you had replaced because experience had taught you they were too dangerous or too painful to maintain. It was suggested parenthetically at the end of young Sam's soccer story that someday, if he were to become more fully alive and mature, he would need to reclaim the self awareness and spontaneity that he gave up that day when he unconsciously decided it was too dangerous to share his excitement.

Why might stretching be mistaken for sacrificing, which is a form of self-abuse? Because both are uncomfortable. Stretching is uncomfortable because the fear that motivated us to discontinue the behavior in the first place will resurface as we risk reclaiming the "dangerous" behavior (which, in Sam's case was spontaneously sharing his excitement). However, behaving in ways that are not in our own best interest is also uncomfortable. There is a different quality to the discomfort of stretching versus the discomfort of self-sacrifice, but each of us has to learn through self-observation how to distinguish the difference.

One formula I can give you to make this distinction is this: We each have within us an "aliveness barometer," an internal measure of our pulsing motion. To "read" your barometer to determine if you are stretching or sacrificing, you must pay attention to your body. If the discomfort is accompanied by your feeling lighter and more vibrant, even if for a brief moment, you are stretching. Conversely, if your discomfort feels heavy, energy depleting, and depressed, you are sacrificing. Take this reading after risking the stretch, not during the stretch.

You'll also find yourself becoming more proficient in discerning what is growth-producing and what is destructive by remembering that criticism is always destructive. Recognizing criticism and disallowing it in your life, whether it comes from yourself or from others, will take you a long way toward healthier relationships and personal growth.

This short story will demonstrate criticism as a destructive presence in a relationship:

> Martha and Mark had been married for less than three years. He controlled the purse strings of their finances. Though both of their names were on the checkbook, Martha didn't write a check until she had cleared it with Mark. She had learned through experience that risking the expenditure wasn't worth the price of his demeaning and criticizing her. He, on the other hand, wrote checks whenever he liked (never consulting Martha). However, Mark had all the responsibility for paying bills and making sure that the well never ran dry. If money was short, it was his fault—and Martha let him know it. Any financial discussion between them turned almost immediately into an argument.

The result of this arrangement was that Martha resented Mark because she saw him as a tyrant with all the power who wouldn't let her have a voice in financial decisions. And Mark resented Martha because he saw her as irresponsible and selfish, while he felt constantly burdened with the full responsibility for keeping their financial boat afloat. So each of them was critical of the other, and felt they were sacrificing because the other was "getting the better end of the deal." Each felt the balance was off in favor of the other.

Interestingly, as it turns out, each was receiving an unconscious payoff. Mark was in control, and Martha was taken care of financially. But the price felt greater than the benefit, which is, of course, why each felt s/he was sacrificing in the relationship.

When you attempt to feel good about yourself through self-sacrifice—attempting to fill another's need through depriving yourself—you are not only denying your needs and being unaware of your real motivation, you are also being manipulative, encouraging over-dependence or selfishness, and instilling guilt or entitlement. This is not a loving gift. Attempting to do another's part for them in relationship, as in life, is ultimately disrespectful of him/her and of you. Neither party benefits. This out-of-balance dynamic will continue to be a source of conflict until both you and your partner can risk stretching beyond your dysfunctional adaptive behaviors.

Back to Mark and Martha's situation. What might stretching be for each of them?

Generally speaking, Mark rationalizes that Martha is not capable of making smart financial decisions, so he is "protecting" her by monopolizing the financial reins. He needs to stretch into being more respectful and less intrusive by letting go and sharing financial decision-making and responsibility with her. Only Martha can tell Mark exactly what behaviors on his part would do that.

On the other hand, Martha rationalizes that "leaving" Mark in control of the finances makes him feel important and manly. She needs to stretch into being more supportive and appreciative of Mark by telling him he's doing a good job and letting him know she appreciates his handling this responsibility. Only Mark can determine the exact behaviors that would provide that for him.

By eliminating criticism, sharing their desires clearly with one another, and replacing their own rationalizations about the other with their partner's self-revelations, Martha and Mark will become more respectful and trusting of each other. Both will be happier and their lives together will be more loving.

Learning which of your needs must be met by another and which must be realized on your own will be a natural by-product of your developmental process.

You can count on the fact that meeting your partner's legitimate intimacy needs will never require you to alter your real Self. If you are thinking "Oh, yeah?" the possibility is fairly good that you have been conditioned to indulge in self-sacrificial behaviors that you have mistakenly thought were your duty as a loving partner. Remember the importance of learning to distinguish between stretching and sacrificing. If you are psychologically poorer as the result of what you are gifting your partner, stop! What you are doing is *not* stretching.

The behavior that you'll have to alter to meet your partner's needs will always be adaptive behavior; you'll never need to forfeit wholesome behavior. Nonetheless, releasing behaviors that seem necessary to your well-being is terrifying. Adaptive behavior *feels* instinctive. Difficulty, and at times unwillingness, to give it up is absolutely understandable. But on those occasions when you repeat your adaptive behaviors, both you and your partner will be further damaged. The same applies for your partner's management of their adaptive behaviors. This is the lose/lose potential.

Remembering the following rule of thumb will help you increase the likelihood of win/win outcomes:

Generally, the person inclined to minimize will need their partner to decrease demands (nagging or controlling), and provide more freedom and/or space by helping with "chores." A "Minimizer" feels loved when you honor their uniqueness and free them of burdensome responsibility.

The person inclined to maximize will need more attention, closeness, and interactive time with their partner. The

"Maximizer" feels loved when you take time from other activities to give your undivided attention to being involved with and responsive to them.

However, so as not to get stuck in stereotyping and labeling, remember that all of us need attention when we are feeling alone and help when we are feeling overwhelmed with responsibilities. Regaining the balance is what's important. Notice that in intimate relationships, there are no win/lose scenarios. The outcome for one is the outcome for both. Learning how to be in the relationship so that both benefit is the goal.

Now that you know your heart's desires, you are in position to respectfully request the changes that you need from your partner so that those desires can be realized. Three basic guidelines for learning to structure such communications, called *Behavior Change Requests*, follow.

STRUCTURING BEHAVIOR CHANGE REQUESTS

GUIDELINE I

Conscious focus and persistence is required to form a *Behavior Change Request*. Remind yourself to stay focused— not on what you don't want—but on what you *do* want (your desire) that is within your partner's "stretch-ability." Translate each block of criticism and complaining that appears as your partner's adaptive behavior from Step III into a phrase that describes the behavior that, if you got it, would meet your need and/or fulfill your desire to some degree. Write it down in this form:

> "Rather than (<u>item from my list</u>), what I would like is for (<u>my partner</u>) to (<u>state specific behavior that meets need</u>). This will satisfy my desire/need for (<u>unmet need from childhood</u>) which I did not experience sufficiently in my childhood."

This procedure typically requires trial-and-error experimenting to discover what will really meet the need or fulfill the desire.

> Example: "Rather than John's <u>being late for an appointment with me</u> , what I would like is for him <u>to arrive at the time that he said he would, or call me and let me know that he's running late as soon as he realizes that he's not going to be on time</u> . This will satisfy my desire <u>to feel valued and respected</u> which I did not experience sufficiently in my childhood."

Translating this example into a Behavior Change Request is simple—do *not* mention what you don't want or what you aren't getting. Stating how the requested behavior will satisfy your unmet childhood needs is optional.

> Example of a Behavior Change Request: "John, I would like you to arrive at the time that you say, or call and let

me know that you're running late as soon as you realize that you're not going to be on time."

GUIDELINE II

The three characteristics of a workable Behavior Change Request are:

1. The statement is positive. That is, the request is for something that the partner will *do*, rather than for something that the partner will stop doing.
2. The statement requests concrete behaviors, rather than abstract generalizations.
3. The statement is clear and specific (quantified and qualified).

Notice that the above example of a Behavior Change Request meets the three criteria:

1. The statement is positive in that John is asked to "arrive at the time you say, or call." (A possible negative request is "Don't be late.")
2. The statement requests a concrete behavior in that John is asked to behave in a particular way: "arrive at the time that you say, or call and let me know that you're running late." (An example of an unacceptable abstract request might be "Have more respect for my time.")
3. And the criterion to be clear and specific is also met: "Arrive at the time you say you will or call and let me know as soon as you realize that you're not going to be on time." (A nonspecific request could be "Get there as soon as you can.")

Learning to craft and deliver—as well as to receive and grant—clear Behavior Change Requests is an essential skill in your pursuit of a loving relationship that will last a lifetime.

GUIDELINE III

Write this sentence:

- If you are presently in a significant love relationship:

  "I pledge to myself that, when I experience *reactivity* with (my partner), the content of my communication will focus more and more on what I need and want in the moment and less and less on what I do not like or want. I am committed to eliminating criticism and complaining from my life and replacing them with Behavior Change Requests."   (Sign name.)

- If you are not presently in a significant love relationship:

  "I am committed to eliminating criticism and complaining from my life and replacing them with Behavior Change Requests. Even though I do not have a partner committed to do this process with me at this time, I will, nonetheless, intentionally practice the skill of crafting Behavior Change Requests in selected interactions with others in my life."   (Sign name.)

Now, write the statement of your commitment at least three times.

Entering the Awareness Stage is not an automatic, preprogrammed happening as is entry into the first two stages, Romantic Love and the Power Struggle. Specific, intentional choices and behaviors are required to move beyond the Power Struggle. There is no free ticket to awareness. A common entry for many couples is psychotherapy or marriage counseling. By reading the preceding chapters, learning the concepts presented in the "Make It Known" sections, and doing the exercises in the "Make It Personal" sections, you are learning more about loving relationships.

As you follow the instructions in "Discovering the Key to Your Heart" and "How to Work with Keys So That Both Hearts Open to Healing and Growing," you are learning more about yourself and your partner (or potential partner). Unbeknown to you, if you have completed Steps I through V and Guidelines I through III, you are already into the third stage of creating a mature, lasting love relationship: The Awareness Stage.

Congratulations! You are well on your way toward the relationship of your dreams.

Make It Known

1. Real love becomes possible only as each partner freely chooses to *give* the other the key to his/her heart. The key is what you need to feel loved.

2. Only as you discover what your needs are, and reveal them in a way that your partner can know them, does the possibility exist that your needs will ever be met. And vice versa. If each partner decides to use the other's *key* by gifting them accordingly, each can become healed and whole, and together they can create an intimate, mature love relationship.

3. Creating a "happily-ever-after" requires sufficient information, time, effort, and commitment to both discovering the key to each other's heart, and learning the process of how to work with each of your keys so that both hearts open to healing and to growing.

4. The first two stages of intimate relationships, Romantic Love and the Power Struggle, are natural stages in that they occur automatically because they are driven by our past.

5. The three potential stages of intimate relating— Awareness, Transformation, and Real Love—are not automatic stages. They become possible only as we develop both by learning specific kinds of information about ourselves, about our partner, and about loving relationships, and by consciously and intentionally applying this information as we learn valuable interpersonal relationship skills.

6. The process of discovering where your and your partner's

wounds are, and learning what behaviors will be required for each of you to heal and grow, is called the Awareness Stage—the third stage of a primary intimate relationship.

7. To even consider that the very qualities that you find unacceptable in your partner really live, denied and disowned, within yourself is a quantum leap in consciousness.

8. In order to grow beyond self-hatred, or to state it positively, to grow into loving yourself, you must be willing to probe within, discover your deepest wounds, and acknowledge the destructive effects of your adaptive behavior.

9. The next step is choosing to forsake your adaptive behaviors. However, there will be times when your reactivity is so intense, you'll be unable to stop its replaying.

10. If, in spite of your fears, you shore yourself up and summon the courage to risk becoming vulnerable, it will be the most potentially healing and growth-producing step that you will ever take.

11. Identifying where you are wounded allows you to determine precisely what you need that you did not historically receive. It is your responsibility to tell your partner exactly what the needed behavior is, and s/he must be willing to stretch and give it to you. This allows you to feel loved and lovable in the parts of yourself that were previously alienated, thereby releasing your self-hatred.

12. You must be willing to stretch into meeting your partner's needs as well. The process is possible only when both do it. Healing and being healed requires two active and involved players.

13. Mature, loving partners are committed to the total welfare of one another.

14. As you discover the specific nurturing behaviors that you

require to be healed, or to feel loved, you'll have identified the very behaviors that your partner needs to develop to become a more mature and whole person. And your partner's healing will require from you the behaviors that you need to develop within yourself so that you can be more mature and whole.

15. Becoming vulnerable is a prerequisite to becoming intimate. Asking for what you need, and being available to receive it if your partner chooses to give it to you, feels terribly risky, just as it feels risky to open yourself to giving what your partner needs.

16. It takes two people in cooperative effort to open each other's heart. Each provides the key to their own dark places, and the other turns the key in the lock and gently lets the light illuminate the darkness.

17. You give up criticism, all the various forms of your adaptive behavior, by replacing it with saying what you desire.

18. Developing your capacity to distinguish between healthy stretching and unhealthy self-sacrifice is essential for your well-being. You can count on the fact that meeting your partner's legitimate intimacy needs will never require you to alter your real Self. Only your adaptive behaviors will need to be altered.

19. In intimate relationships, there are no win/lose scenarios. The outcome for one is the outcome for both. Learning how to be in the relationship so that both benefit, is the goal.

20. For your partner to be able to meet your needs, s/he needs to know which aspects of her/his adaptive behaviors are re-wounding you—causing you pain. And, of course, the same is true of you. Both of you need information about the specific behaviors you must stretch into.

21. Three basic guidelines in learning how to structure Behavior Change Requests, the communication of your desires to your partner, follow:

    Guideline I: Conscious focus and persistence is required to form a Behavior Change Request.

    Guideline II: The three characteristics of a workable Behavior Change Request are:

        i. The statement is positive.

        ii. The statement requests concrete behaviors.

        iii. The statement is clear and specific.

    Guideline III: To yourself, pledge that you are committed to eliminating criticism and complaining from your life by replacing them with Behavior Change Requests.

Make It Personal

Much of this chapter is devoted to your gathering personal information, which is the essence of the Awareness Stage. Doing the exercises within the chapter will give you the necessary information to create a mature and lasting love relationship.

Stage Four: Transformation 7

The witch's spell is broken

Come live with me, and be my love,
And we will some new pleasures prove
Of golden sands, and crystal brooks,
With silken lines, and silver hooks.

> —John Donne, The Bait
> *The Compleat Angler*, 1653

THE HANDSOME PRINCE RISKED ASKING FOR WHAT he needed to reach Rapunzel. She chose, in spite of her fear, to make herself vulnerable and honor his request. Only when she did what he asked, let her hair down, could the gap between them be bridged and the healing connection made.

For as Rapunzel experienced the handsome Prince risking his life to rescue her, she could no longer see herself as ugly. She could not deny her personal worth without denying the worth of the handsome prince. That would be like Groucho Marx's classic comedic line: "I do not care to belong to a club that accepts people like me as a member." After both risked meeting the other's need, they came close enough to see their beauty mirrored in the eyes of the other. The witch's spell was broken.

You have been learning about your areas of incomplete growth and development, and about what you need from your partner to be healed. This unfinished business from childhood is your relational baggage, which you now know is the root cause of the issues that repeatedly cause pain in your relationships.

There is only one way to rid yourself of that baggage: to commit to doing the work that heals your wounds. By now, you have a good idea of where your wounds are, and what behaviors you need from your partner. You also have information about your partner's wounds, and what behaviors s/he needs from you. You are gaining an appreciation of the difficulty each of you face in stretching to meet one another's needs.

Although this process is not easy, it is the only way to reach real love; there are no shortcuts, no quick fixes, no easy solutions. However, before long you will begin to see results—the transformation of your relationship. In fact, if you have begun effectively using Behavior Change Requests, you're already seeing positive results. This is only a taste of what's to come.

Real love, your goal, means valuing and treasuring one another enough to express your innermost vulnerabilities, and to compassionately hear those of your partner. It means consciously and willingly gifting one another with what they need, and eventually doing so because you genuinely want to. After a while, these behaviors become so much a part of you that doing them is as natural as breathing.

When you and your partner begin consciously and intentionally *applying* what you're learning, the transformation of your relationship is set in motion. The words to this song poetically express this transforming experience:

I remember well the day we wed
I can see that picture in my head
I still believe the words we said forever will ring true.
Love is certain, love is kind, love is yours, and love is mine
But it isn't something that we find, it's something that we
    do.

Holding tight and letting go, flying high and laying low
Let your strongest feelings show and your weakness too.
It's a little and a lot to ask
An endless and a welcome task
Love isn't something that we have, it's something that we
    do.

We have to make each other all that we can be
We can find our strength and inspiration independently.
The way we work together is what sets our love apart
So closely that we can't tell where I end and where you
    start.

It hits me hard remembering how we started with a simple
    vow
There's so much to look back on now, still it feels
    brand new.

We're on a road that has no end
And each day we begin again.
Love's not just something that we're in, it's something
    that we do.

Love is wide and love is long, love is weak and love is
    strong.
Love is why I love this song, I hope you love it too.
I remember well the day we wed
I can see that picture in my head.
Love isn't just the words we said, it's something that we
    do.

There is no request too big or small
We give ourselves, we give our all.
Love isn't someplace that we fall, it's something that we
    do.

—Clint Black and Skip Ewing
"*Something That We Do*"
Nothin' But the Tail Lights (1997)

Are you ready to create your mature, loving relationship? As the song reiterates: "Love isn't someplace that we fall, it's something that we do." Only you can choose your path. This is no time to fool yourself. Nor is it a time to tell your partner what s/he wants to hear just to avoid conflict. Each of you has the right and the responsibility to make your own decision, and to communicate it clearly and respectfully to the other.

If you find yourself wanting and trying to do the work and your partner is persistently unwilling, it may be time to let go. Because unless both of you are doing the work of intimacy building, after a time, continuing to try will result in a self-sacrificial and abusive partnership. This dynamic is lose/lose.

I have come to believe that a wholesome reason for dissolving an intimate love relationship is if you or your partner is unwilling to do the work. Reminding yourself that each of you has the right to make his/her own choices may help you through this difficult time. The more you can honor your differences, without judging one of you as being right and the other as being wrong, the less damaging the dissolution of your partnership will be. If this is your situation, your happily-ever-after will have to come with someone else. The good news is that the time and effort you've extended in personal work on yourself and the relationship isn't wasted. Growth and development aren't lost—you're just that much ahead of the game in whatever comes next in your life.

Couples that commit to do the work, and to do it with one another, are on the threshold of discovering intimacy beyond their imagination. The healing that occurs as you begin to communicate with one another in a healing and growth-producing manner is called *Transformation*, and is the fourth stage of intimate relationships.

We are reminded in the following poem that *how* we communicate our messages—the "music" (tone of voice, inflection, body language, eye contact, etc.)—is at least as significant as what we say:

"You want to know what really bugs me?" he asked.
Sure. What really bugs you?

"It really bugs me when a man
Calls a woman a broad. . . ."

Not me.
You can call me a broad
If you do it with love.
It is the words without love that bug me.
I am bugged by Husbands who say Dear
With the same tenderness they accord the dentist.
I am bugged by Telephone operators who say
Honey
To every party on the line.
I am bugged by Doormen who say
Madam
With contempt in their eyes.
Politeness without patience.
Words without music.
Touch without feel.
That's what bugs this broad.

—Lois Wyse,
A Weeping Eye Can Never See (1972)

Does this "broad's" succinct description of dissonance in personal encounters strike a resonating chord? ". . . Words without music. Touch without feel . . ."

What the woman in the poem calls "music" is referred to in psychological literature as "interpersonal skills." Massive amounts of research and clinical observation have shown that three such skills are necessary in mutually beneficial relationships—*empathy, respect*, and *authenticity*. And the three are defined as follows:

- *Empathy*: Understanding an Other's thoughts and feelings from *their* perspective.
- *Respect*: Concern, regard, and appreciation for the Other's experiences, feelings, and potential.
- *Authenticity*: Expressing One's truth in an appropriate and constructive manner.

These three interpersonal skills, *empathy, respect*, and *authenticity (ERA)*, when clearly communicated between two individuals, add the "spirit" necessary for intimacy building. We must develop these skills if we are ever to have meaningful and wholesome relationships. They not only infuse our words with meaning, they sensitize us in the careful selection of words. The mood that we communicate is composed of words *with* music, touch *with* feel. And for a message to be clear and believable, the music must match the words, and the words must match the music. When they don't, we know. And we, like the woman in the poem, are "bugged."

How do you develop these interpersonal skills? How do you enter *The New ERA of Intimacy?*

Empathy

The basic skill on which the other two rest is *empathy*—understanding an Other's thoughts and feelings from their perspective. The tough part of being empathic is the "from *their* perspective" part.

As a human being, over 99% of our DNA exactly matches the DNA of every other human being (which is no doubt why we are capable of empathy in the first place). It is the remaining less than one percent that makes being empathic difficult. Intentionally letting go of our own perspective is essential if we are to truly hear an Other. The way to accomplish this skill is to focus on the Other and pay attention to them with an open mind.

Matthew Fox, prolific author and educator, said in a keynote address to a group of professional therapists in October of 1996: "Paying attention is the discipline required to experience the divine and the sacred. The reason that we are a-spiritual is that we take for granted." A similar emphasis is made by Dan Millman, author of *Way of the Peaceful Warrior,* in an address at the Maui Writers Conference in September, 1998: "There's God and then there's *not paying attention.*"

Many of us have inadequately developed paying-attention muscles because we are self-absorbed with our own thoughts, interpretations, values, biases, and reactivity, and because we, in our own histories, were not paid attention to. Focusing our full attention on an Other moves us beyond self-absorption. This means that during the moments that we are focusing on our partner, we are not thinking, analyzing, comparing, or second-guessing them. And we cannot possibly be reactive because we are not focusing on ourselves. We are, instead, caught up in *their* world.

Our partners tell us about themselves in so many ways: in how they move their bodies and hold themselves, in how they look or don't look at us, with their facial expressions and tones of voice, by what they say and don't say. To the degree that we are curious, open, and available (*paying attention*) we will "get" what is being sent.

But we cannot maintain this posture independent of the message we are receiving. In other words, what is sent influences our ability to stay open and pay attention so that we *can* "get it." Words are impacting. Whoever wrote "Sticks and stones can break my bones, but words can never harm me," must have been stating a wish, for clearly it is not a reality. Words as well as attitudes can communicate blame, shame, judgment, manipulation, and disrespect. All are forms of criticism that will automatically trigger reactivity in us, making our staying open impossible. Even when your partner has good intentions and is kind-spirited, if s/he inadvertently uses a word, phrase, or nonverbal gesture that has pejorative implications for you, a threatening message will be received.

You cannot get away from the fact that as a human being, you have a history that operates at an unconscious level to influence how you presently experience yourself and others. Evolving beyond the limitations imposed by your history requires the cooperation of both you and your partner.

Your being more actively conscious of this phenomenon allows you, when you are communicating, to choose your words and your nonverbal behaviors more carefully. Also, if you're not getting through to your partner, check your own heart for the possibility of self-sabotaging feelings and/or actions. If you discover negative feelings, just acknowledging and reporting them to your partner is helpful.

Both persons interact to create an increasingly empathic encounter, or a decreasingly empathic encounter. You communicate empathy with your words and with your "music." The more precisely you match the words, tone, energy, expressions, inflections, and gestures of your partner—the more they will feel understood. Being understood is, by the way, a basic human need. (Being able *to* understand is also a basic human need—and when you are empathic, you derive this side benefit.) Without this experience of understanding, you feel crazy.

But empathy alone is not enough for a healing growth

encounter. The other two interpersonal skills, respect and authenticity, must also be in place in order for empathy to be optimally wholesome.

Respect

Respect is the second interpersonal skill essential for intimacy building. Respecting another person means having caring, concern, regard, and appreciation for their feelings, potentials, and experiences. It means holding the other's point of view equal to your own. This eliminates the inclination to persuade, convince, or in any way attempt to proselytize the other. Who is "right," a major source of conflict for many, does not exist as an issue. Even when perspectives are quite different, and therefore not equally preferred, they can still be equally respected.

To respect another's outlook as valid doesn't necessarily mean that we agree with them, just that we acknowledge that theirs is a reasonable way to see the world. Agreement isn't necessary for validation when a respectful attitude is in place. What may result from mutually regarding one another's opinions is a third, perhaps more inclusive view. Or each partner may continue to hold his/her own separate perspective. The point is that no one is trying to manipulate the other. Rather, each supports the other's right to his/her individual reality and choices.

Authenticity

The third interpersonal skill is *authenticity*, the expression of one's truth in an appropriate and constructive manner. And it is mentioned third for good reason. Without the first two, empathy and respect, authenticity is impossible. How do we determine what's appropriate? And why would we want to be constructive? Because we are becoming more understanding and more caring of the Other.

It is important to recognize that authenticity is not synonymous with honesty. We've all heard people say, "Well, to be honest with you. . . ." Better put on your hard-hat, right? What is apt to follow is blunt criticism. "The truth, the whole truth, and nothing but the truth" is *not* the definition of authenticity.

Before being "totally honest" with somebody, check inside yourself to see if you're being empathic and respectful. Of course, whatever you *do* say must be accurate and from your core. The test is to ask yourself, "Is this *really* my truth, my reality, *underneath* my fear?" Authenticity comes from the soul, the very essence of you.

When you put words to your defenses, the things you say because you're scared and alienated, it comes out as criticism, judgment, or manipulation. Notice that this is adaptive behavior and therefore not authentic communication. If you're not sure whether a thought or feeling is coming from defensiveness, leaving it unexpressed (at least until you get more clarity) may be the wholesome choice.

When you're being authentic, you will be selective in what you say, leaving unsaid anything that is not relevant or is not mutually beneficial. Being clear that you are speaking only from your limited perspective and opinion is another hallmark of authenticity.

A responsible communication will be prefaced with something like "I think . . ." "It seems to me . . ." "I feel . . ." or "My perception is . . ." For instance: "I have the feeling that you don't like what I'm wearing," is something you can know with certainty. "You don't like what I'm wearing" is *not* something you can know.

Learning that you cannot speak for another—not just because it's thoughtless or rude, but because you truly cannot *know* another's truth—is an awareness that comes with maturing.

You also show a lack of empathy and respect for your partner when you do not say your authentic truth. Believing that you must protect yourself or your partner suggests that you neither trust yourself nor him/her. The vulnerability necessary for intimacy building comes from opening to hear your partner's reality so that you can know him/her, and saying what you mean so that your partner can know you.

It is not difficult to see that all three interpersonal skills—empathy, respect and authenticity—are necessary in making real love happen. And together they are incorporated into a transforming process known as "The ERA Process" (charts printed on pages 162-163).

This procedure has evolved over many years of my working with individuals and couples. It synthesizes other forms of dialogue, interweaving the transforming attributes from each, and incorporating them into a single structure.

When you see the steps that constitute The ERA Process, it looks simple. It looks like nothing more than a communication technique. And it is a communication technique. But it is far *more. It is a highly structured communicative process that promotes intimacy as well as personal growth and development.*

When you and your partner are having a problem, the obvious

may be to conclude, as did the character in the movie *Cool Hand Luke,* that "What we have here is a failure to communicate." However, it is important to recognize that significant conflict in relationships is not just the result of ". . . a failure to communicate;" rather, relationship issues are caused by developmental issues.

Understanding the power of this process is easy. The ERA Process provides a clear format that assures, as you become more adept through practice, that you and a partner are protecting balanced pulsing in your relationship. There is equal sending (pulsing out) and equal receiving (pulsing in). No one is intruding; no one is neglecting. Each is communicating by word and action: "I'm noticing the contours of your space and am precise as I pour myself into you—careful that I neither pour too little (to starve you) nor too much (to drown you)."

It isn't vital that you grasp the reality of the pulsing function in order to do the work, in the same vein that you don't have to understand *why* a medication or prescription cures your ills in order for it to be effective. But you do need to *take the prescription* or *do it* in order for promised results to come about.

The ERA Process, when engaged skillfully, keeps both partners safe and open so that they truly *see* and *hear* themselves and the other. Reactivity will not be present, for they will each experience mutual understanding (Empathy), caring (Respect), and full permission to be genuine (Authenticity). Time and again, I have seen couples flourish in one another's presence as they become inhabitants of *The New ERA of Intimacy.* And those who persevere and become skillful create a mature, loving relationship.

The ERA Process™

*A highly structured communicative process that promotes intimacy
as well as personal growth and development.*

The ERA Process is increasingly realized as **both participants** experience and demonstrate to one another greater degrees of the interpersonal skills of Empathy, Respect and Authenticity (ERA).

[**Empathy**: Understanding an Other's thoughts and feelings from their communicated perspective.]

[**Respect**: Concern, regard, and appreciation for the Other's experiences, feelings, and potential.]

[**Authenticity**: Expression of One's "truth" in an appropriate and constructive manner.]

"The ERA Process" requires **two active roles**:
One is Sending, the Other is Receiving.
In these roles, each intentionally "gifts" the other.

[Intentionality is counter-instinctive and can be extremely threatening.]

THE PROCESS

SENDING	RECEIVING
① <u>Request appointment</u> to engage in "The ERA Process."	**②** <u>Grant a time</u> as soon as possible.
③ <u>Notice</u> your authentic "truth" within at this very moment.	**③** Turn off self awareness and <u>be</u> totally curious, open, and <u>attentive</u> to Sender.
⑤ <u>Report</u> clearly what you notice within yourself so that you are increasingly transparent and available to be known by the Receiver.	**④** Invite the Sender to "send" by saying, **"<u>I am available to hear you.</u>"**
⑦ <u>Add information</u> that comes to you until you have stated all of the pieces in your awareness on the subject. When invited to say more, and there is no more new data coming into your awareness, report **"<u>That is all there is about that for now</u>"** and stop.	**⑥** When Sender pauses, <u>Mirror</u> precisely what you have heard and seen (content, tone of voice, pace and intensity of delivery, body language, etc.) and ask **"<u>Did I get it?</u>"** If the answer is "Yes," invite the Sender to **"<u>Tell me more.</u>"** If the answer is "No," say **"<u>Tell me what I missed,</u>"** then Mirror. Re-invite **"<u>Tell me more.</u>"**
⑨ When asked if Receiver got it all, <u>Respond with missing pieces</u> until you can honestly say **"<u>You got it.</u>"** If, in the validation statement, the Receiver misses accurate feelings, <u>Offer corrections</u>. When Receiver makes corrections, say **"<u>You got it.</u>"**	**⑧** When the Sender reports "That's all," do a <u>Summary Mirror</u>, followed by **"<u>Did I get it all?</u>"** If Sender makes corrections, <u>Mirror</u>, until Sender says "You got it." Send a validating statement: **"<u>You make sense to me, and given all of that, I can imagine you might feel (state appropriate feelings).</u>"** If Sender makes corrections, Mirror until Sender says "You got it."
⑩ Take a deep, audible breath.	**⑩** Take a deep, audible breath.
⑪ Exchange roles.	**⑪** Exchange roles.

Helpful Hints for Self Monitoring "The ERA Process"

INDICATORS OF NOT BEING IN THE PROCESS

WHEN SENDING

- The Sender is **Being Critical.**

  Examples:

Blaming	"You started it!"
Shaming	"I can't believe you stole my one opportunity."
Judging	"Anyone who would do a thing like that is weird."

- The Sender is **Attempting to Manipulate an Outcome.**

  Examples:

Being Selective	"I bought your dinner twice this week." (Fails to mention that you bought her lunch 3 times last week.)
Is Unclear	"That is an epistemological methodology of thinking." (Purposely uses words and abstractions that are unknown to you.)
Exaggerating/ Minimizing	"You are only interested in yourself - everything for Mary and no thought about anybody else." (Paints a distorted picture by inaccurate emphasis.)

- The Sender is **Making Assumptions that s/he knows the Receiver's "truth."**

  Examples:

"I-Know-You"	Any "You" statement, such as "You always liked him better."
"I-Know-You-Better-Than-You-Know-You"	"What you really mean is you don't want to do it."

WHEN RECEIVING

- The Receiver is **Demonstrating Reactivity** because s/he is focused on Self rather than on Sender.

  Examples:

  Self-absorbed crying, frowning, audibly sighing, intentionally looking away, crossing arms, rolling eyes, shaking head, glaring, and verbally interrupting.

- The Receiver is **Thinking.**

  Examples:

Analyzing	Thinking "You just don't want to take me out to dinner because you are in a hurry to get home to watch the ball game."
Interpreting	Thinking "You're only saying that to me because I remind you of your mother."

- The Receiver is **Being Inattentive to the Sender** in other ways.

  Examples:

Distracted	Daydreaming, watching TV, reading. (Becoming engrossed in something other than the Sender's immediate "send.")
Interrupting	Blurting out, "That's not the way I remember it!"
Has difficulty Mirroring	Mirrors inaccurately or incompletely.

INTERNAL DYNAMICS OF BEING IN THE PROCESS

WHEN SENDING

The Sender is **Being Authentic.**
This exists when the Sender is expressing his/her "truth" in an appropriate and constructive manner.

The Sender is **Being Respectful.**
This occurs when Sender is aware that his/her "truth" is limited by personal perspective, and communicates this awareness by using "I" statements only. The Sender is eager to be known even at the risk of being vulnerable.

WHEN RECEIVING

The Receiver is **Being Empathic.**
This is accomplished by the Receiver paying full attention to the Sender. The Receiver's attentiveness is driven by his/her desire to understand the Sender's perspective.

The Receiver is **Being Respectful.**
This manifests when the Receiver is being nonjudgmental, open, eager to receive, curious and vulnerable.

Each of us is instrumental in making it possible for the Other to stay in the Process.
We *Are* One Another's Context!

There are two active roles in The ERA Process: one is *sending*, the other is *receiving*. These terms, *sending* and *receiving,* simply refer to the acts of doing the communicating (talking and gesturing) and receiving the communication (listening and observing). The person who is talking and gesturing is the Sender, and the one who is listening and observing is the Receiver. You will take turns filling each of these roles.

When you notice that something is bothering you and you'd like your partner to understand or hear you, ask for an appointment to do The ERA Process. Each partner has not only the right, but also the responsibility to address relationship issues in this way. By doing so, you demonstrate your commitment to your relationship and to your growth and healing.

If I were sitting down with you and your partner for the first time to begin learning this process, I would tell you that there are ways to make it easier until you become more skilled. Here are a few points I would make:

- To do this process, there must be *two* people who are choosing to take responsibility for doing their part. Neither partner is to try to cajole the other into doing it.

- This procedure is very specific. In the beginning, neither you nor your partner will be able to maintain the structure exactly as it is designated, *but do the very best that you can.* Because the more exactly each of you stick to the directions, the more benefit each of you will derive. In fact, *not* doing the process as indicated, could result in another wounding experience.

- Know up front that this process will seem unnatural,

stilted, and time-consuming. You will not be engaged in a conversation. I cannot recall anyone who, in the beginning, liked doing it (including me!). So if you feel as though you're alternating between being a robot and a parrot, you are probably doing it just right. If you and your partner will stick with it, your experience will change dramatically. The payoff potential is phenomenal.

- Start by communicating about topics that are not particularly controversial between you. (Just as with any new skill you are learning, start with baby steps and gradually move to more advanced work. For instance, if you were training to run a marathon, you wouldn't start the first day by attempting to run the full 26.2 miles.)

- Limit the amount of time that one person is in the "sending" role. Begin with about ten minutes. Then switch roles so that the other person is in the role of Sender for ten minutes. (Equal time in each role is important.)

- Limit each *send*; keeping them to no more than a few sentences at first. When invited to "Tell me more," say another few sentences. This allows you to say what you wish, while giving your partner the opportunity to mirror your *send* in smaller chunks.

- Every time you enter The ERA Process, each partner has the opportunity to be in the role of Sender the same number of times.

- The more often you and your partner engage in the

process, the sooner you'll notice positive results in your relationship. I recommend that you start with twice a week for twenty-minutes with each person sending ten minutes and each receiving ten minutes. As you become more adept, increase the length and the frequency of your "dates" together. Eventually, you will discover that you're both naturally living in the spirit and form of The ERA Process without having to consciously work at it. This is the goal!

By you and your partner disciplining yourselves to be with one another in this new, intentional way, growth and healing is assured. And, when you find yourselves veering from the structure and hurting one another, STOP. Set up a future date to try again *after* each of you has spent some time imagining yourself and the other in a positive light. Be kind and gentle with yourselves. You'll become wholesome inhabitants within *The New ERA* yet. Just don't give up!

—THE ERA PROCESS—

Together, let's walk through the steps of The ERA Process. (From time to time you may want to refer back to the charts printed on pages 162-163.)

Step 1 — *Sender: Request an appointment to engage in* The ERA Process.

Learning to respect another person includes realizing that s/he is not obliged to spend time listening to you whenever you want. Step 1 truly is a request, not a demand. In a clear, respectful manner, say "I'd like an appointment to enter The ERA Process."

Step 2 — *Receiver: Grant a time as soon as possible.*

When your partner requests to engage in The ERA Process, you clearly have a choice to grant or not grant the request. If you are committed to your partner's and to your own growth and healing, as well as to developing a mature intimate relationship, you will choose to grant his/her request "as soon as possible." ("Possible" means when you can both give your undivided attention to the process. Ways to help assure your privacy are to turn off the TV or radio, unplug the phone, agree to ignore the doorbell, and request that others living in the house respect your privacy for the next thirty minutes or so.)

Both of you may be available to give your undivided attention the instant that the request is made. If so, the Receiver says, "I'm available now. Does this time work for you?" And the Sender agrees or not that now is fine.

Or it may be, for example, that the potential Receiver knows that s/he can't possibly focus on this process before the kids are down for the night—in which case, a sample response might be: "I'll be available for The ERA Process as soon as we get the kids in bed this evening, say . . . around eight. How's that for you?"

(It is necessary to negotiate until a mutually agreeable time is found, because doing the process requires both persons' full cooperation and concentration.)

When you've come together at the appointed time, move on to Step 3.

Step 3 — (Receiver and Sender)

Receiver: *Turn off preoccupation with yourself and be totally curious,* open, and attentive to the Sender.

Pay attention to him/her with sitting-on-the-edge-of-your-seat curiosity. Take him/her in with your eyes. Tune your ears solely to his/her frequency. Be engrossed in receiving him/her. Although personal thoughts inevitably seep through cracks in concentration, simply refocus on him/her, allowing introspection no chance for a toehold. The more proficient you are in this process of paying total attention to your partner, the less likely you will become reactive.

Sender: *Focus full attention on yourself in this very moment.*

Closing your eyes to block out external stimulation may make it easier to access your inner world of thoughts and feelings. Go inside yourself and breathe slowly and deeply for several minutes. This will permit superficial and inauthentic thoughts to evaporate.

Step 4 — *Receiver: Invite your partner to send by saying, "I am available to hear you."*

When you have calmed your reactivity as best you can and freed yourself to pay full attention to the Sender, offer in a relaxed, gracious, and unhurried manner, the invitation, "I am available to hear you." Keep your tone of voice relatively low-pitched, mellow, and gentle.

Step 5 — *Sender: Report clearly what you are noticing within yourself so that you are increasingly transparent and known by your partner.*

Express aloud the thoughts and feelings you're experiencing moment by moment. Allow stream-of-consciousness reporting. Maintaining access to your truth requires focus, as your inclination is to fall into the ruts of well-worn, familiar thinking patterns. (Rut thinking is nonproductive because you are not paying attention to yourself in the moment. If you are not engaged with what is real for you in the moment, you cannot engage another. This is disrespectful of both you and your partner.)

Clues that you are voicing rut thinking:

1. You are glib.
2. You've said these words before in just this way (the Receiver hears you as preaching or delivering a speech that s/he has memorized from repeated hearings).
3. Your communication is not producing new insights; rather, both you and the Receiver are bored or reactive.
4. You're not thinking of anything to say.
5. You're monitoring or censoring what you do think of.

6. You're limiting what you say to a minimal number of words.

Overcoming rut thinking requires that you stop, take a breath, tune-in again and express your stream of consciousness.

Rather than delivering a premeditated speech or monitoring what you say, risk forming your sentences as you speak. Self-monitoring is appropriate *only* to eliminate criticizing, manipulating, and messages that assume you know about your partner. In other words, make only "I" statements, and disallow yourself to blame, shame, or judge.

An example: "I'm remembering last night when I waited for you in the restaurant. It's almost like experiencing it all over again. At first, I was excited and looking forward to seeing you. Then I got more and more disappointed every time the door opened and it wasn't you. I felt so taken for granted, sitting there waiting and waiting. As time went by, I felt more and more like our date just wasn't important to you, and I resented that. Finally, I got really angry."

A second example: "I want you to know how much I enjoyed our walk this afternoon. I really am having a lot more fun when we're together than I was there for a while. And I like that. I like that a lot. And I guess I'm wondering how you've felt lately when we're together."

Step 6 — *Receiver: Mirror the Sender precisely—what you are hearing and seeing.* Match the content, tone of voice, pace and intensity of delivery, and body language, then ask, "Did I

get it?" If your partner says "Yes," invite him/ her: "Tell me more." If the answer is "No," say, "Tell me what I missed," and then mirror that piece until your partner says, "You've got it." Let the Sender know you are still open and available to hear them by re-inviting them: "Tell me more."

As the Receiver, your first job is to mirror. Using "mirror" as a verb serves well to communicate the function of receiving. A good mirror has no creative function. It doesn't add to, subtract from, or distort. It simply reflects what's in front of it. This is the value of a mirror—it allows you to see exactly what is there—especially the parts you cannot otherwise see. What a grand function!

In the act of *mirroring*, the Receiver provides this gift of a good mirror. This means you express EXACTLY (yes, the same words with the same tone, pace, and inflection, as well as the same nonverbal behavior—as close to a video recording as you can manage) what the Sender communicates. This does *not* sound or look like mimicking when it's done precisely.

(Although accurate paraphrasing is also fine, I recommend an exact "parroting" initially. As you become more skilled, you will be able to paraphrase accurately.)

You, as the Receiver, will need all of your willpower on board to be able to do this. The more precise the mirroring, the more effective the process.

If through a crack in concentration, you are remembering something different from what the Sender is saying, dismiss your contradictory thoughts, and refocus on the Sender's message.

> For example: Sender says: "All we do is sit home
> and watch TV night after night. I guess I'm just
> going to have to get used to having no social life."

As the Receiver, your memory is that you've repeatedly
attempted to initiate the two of you going out, but s/he always
says s/he's too tired.

> A second example: The Sender says, "You didn't
> tell me you were going out of town next week.
> Here it is Saturday and you casually mention
> that you need me to take you to the airport
> Monday morning. That makes me feel like you
> have no regard for my plans—like yours are
> more important than mine."

Let's pretend that you, the Receiver, remember it very
differently. You're certain that you mentioned your travel
plans at least twice—once the morning you made plane
reservations, and again last week when s/he asked you
about celebrating your son's birthday.

When you're in the role of Receiver, times like these
make it difficult not to become reactive and interrupt. But
remember that *perception* is what is being sent, and the
Sender is the sole authority on their perception.
Interrupting with your version of the event (even when you
are certain that you're right) is contrary to your supportive
role, which is to listen and to hear your partner's experience.
Sometimes it helps to quickly remind yourself that you'll have

an opportunity to say whatever is your perspective in a few minutes when you change roles. Then release your thoughts and focus again on putting yourself in the Sender's skin. Sense what s/he is experiencing.

One way that self-absorption manifests is when the Receiver is intimidated by the task of mirroring, and focuses on *trying to remember* what's being sent. This is counterproductive. *Any* focus other than simply paying attention to the Sender is distracting and will decrease your ability to "get it." The key is in *risking letting go and giving in to being attentive.* When it's time to mirror back, the information will be remarkably available within you.

When the Sender indicates that you "have it," which may be in the form of a nod or gesture, allow no more than five seconds of silence before offering the soft invitation to "Tell me more." (Lean toward the Sender, make eye contact, use a calm tone of voice, and let your voice drop on the word "more.") This invitation must communicate the gentle message "I am open and available to hear all that you wish to say." A hint of anything other than authentic and caring availability, such as a tone of demanding, prying, disinterest or impatience, will trigger reactivity in the Sender.

In the earlier example of a *send*, the last statement, ". . . And I guess I'm wondering how you've felt lately when we're together," sounds like a request for a response from the Receiver. Even if the Sender were to ask a direct question, the Receiver does not reply at the time. The Receiver only *mirrors* what is sent; for example, ". . . And I hear you wondering how I've felt lately when we're together."

When it becomes the Receiver's turn to be the Sender,

s/he has the choice whether to answer or respond to any part of their partner's former *send* as a part of their *send*. There is no obligation. What either person says when they are in the role of the Sender will be determined entirely by what is coming up for them in the moment. *This process is not a conversation. There is no requirement for you to connect your send to that of your partner's previous send.*

Step 7 — ***Sender: When invited to "Tell me more," tune in to your inner thoughts** and feelings, and notice if you have anything more to say. If so, say it. If you have communicated what is important to you (sometimes, less is more), stop. Then say, "That's all there is for now."*

This could sound something like:

"What I'm remembering right now is a time when I was waiting in the cafeteria after school for my mom to pick me up. We always had to wait in the cafeteria when it was raining. All the kids' parents came and got them, and I was left sitting by myself. The teacher finally got tired of waiting and took me home.

"When Mom came to the door she made a big fuss about being really embarrassed because she forgot to check her watch. When the teacher left, Mom said under her breath, 'Anybody can get busy and forget the time,' disappeared into the kitchen, and left me standing alone in the hall."

Pause.

"That's exactly how I felt last night—forgotten and unimportant."

A second example:

"It's like . . . I can't trust my judgment about you anymore.

"I remember your telling me so many times in the past that I've been wrong about what I thought was going on with you, so maybe I'm looking for a reality check or something to see if I'm reading you better.

Also, I really *do* want you to know that I had a good time this afternoon."

Step 8 — *Receiver: Mirror the send and continue to extend the invitation, "Tell me more."* **Mirror what your partner says until s/he tells you "That's all there is about that for now." Then give a brief summary mirror of the total send. Ask, "Did I get your message?" If s/he makes corrections, mirror those, until s/he says, "You got it." Validate your partner by saying something like: "You really make sense to me, and given all of that, I can imagine that you would feel (state appropriate feelings)." If your partner makes corrections, again mirror, until s/he says, "You got it."**

Step 9 — **Sender:** *When your partner asks if s/he got*

**your message, add missing pieces until you
can honestly say, "You got it." If, in the
validation statement, the Receiver mentions a
feeling that you as the Sender don't have, or if
s/he leaves out a feeling you do have, make
corrections. When the Receiver has it, as a
self-acknowledgment and validation, restate
your feelings.**

For example:

> "Yeah, I really do feel unimportant and not
> cared about—really lonely and sad—when I
> wait and wait and nobody comes."

Step 10— *Receiver and Sender: Take a deep audible breath.*

This step is as important as any other. It enables both
you and your partner to conclude a mind set by shifting
into neutral for a few moments of relaxation and "letting
go."

The deep audible breath prepares the body and mind
to shift into the frame of mind of the new role. That is,
the one who has been taking in (receiving) will shift
into giving out (sending), and vice versa.

Breathing is the ultimate analogy and reality that
reminds us of our pulsing nature. Our very life depends
on balancing the coming-in with the going-out—the
inhaling with the exhaling. Just as our bodies require this
balance, good relationships also require this balance. That's

why it's so important that we spend approximately equal time sending and receiving, and that we experience as much time paying attention as being paid attention to.

Step 11 — *Receiver and Sender: Exchange roles and repeat the process.*

Recall that this process is not a conversation. When the roles reverse, the new Sender has absolute choice in what s/he sends. There is no obligation, requirement, or expectation that the former Sender's topic is going to be pursued, although it may be. It all depends on what comes up when the sender checks in with her/himself.

Each time you engage in this process, allow both partners to have an equal number of times in the sending and receiving roles. This ensures the experience of reciprocity.

At the conclusion of The ERA Process exercise, the Sender may craft a *Behavior Change Request* and offer it. You'll remember from our discussion in the latter part of Chapter 6 that a *Behavior Change Request* is exactly what the term implies— *requesting* someone to change a behavior in a specific way. This is not a demand; it's simply saying what you would like. If the Receiver is agreeable to granting the request, great! If not, the Receiver states that they are not willing to grant the behavior, and s/he offers an alternative that they *are* willing to grant. The request is then negotiated. This is a skill that requires practice. It replaces criticizing in that, rather than your saying what you do *not* want, you say in specific, positive, and behavioral terms, what you *do* want. By doing this, you will have handed your partner the key to your heart.

An example:

"I'd like you to drive within the speed limit when I'm in the car with you; otherwise, I get scared." (Notice that this is far more respectful than "If you don't stop driving like a maniac, I am never going to get in the car with you again!")

Behavior—ours as well as our partner's, must change in specific ways for growth and healing to occur, and for love to mature.

The behavior changes required as you follow The ERA Process will take you a long way toward meeting your partner's needs. But when you intentionally alter your behavior in the specific ways your partner requests, the maturing process will be accelerated for both of you. Because the very behaviors that your partner needs to feel safe (not threatened, and therefore not reactive) are the same behaviors that you need to develop to become a more mature adult. (Refer to Chapters 3 and 4 if you need to refresh your memory of the *Intimate Partner Profile* Match phenomenon.)

Initially, as you struggle with the process, you may not see the relevance of this time-consuming, stilted and unnatural way of interacting. You may become frustrated and doubt the potential benefit. It doesn't matter. Recall that you're entering a new era. *All that matters is that you do it.*

The ERA Process is a precise roadmap for your journey toward happily-ever-after. Simple? Absolutely. So simple that the potential power in this process can be discounted because it appears *too* simple. Easy? Hardly.

Why is the process so difficult, given that it looks so simple?

In a sentence, it's difficult because we are unfinished creatures, in all the ways we have read about. Your problems in relating to one another, in communicating with one another, and in loving one another and yourself, are a result of the developing you have yet to do and the wounding that has yet to be healed.

Simply being able to identify your wounds does not alter the recordings stored in your body. *Experiencing something different* does. In much the same way that recordings are enhanced by dubbing in music or extra voices, your past history can be enhanced (healed) by getting those needs met that were not met in your past. The mind accesses the old experiences and overlays them with the new. This is psychological healing—regression working in service of wholesomeness.

An Intimate Partner Profile Match partner is the perfect person to heal you, because the unconscious part of you has already accepted her/him as the early caregiver from whom your major wounds came. Perfect! The unconscious opens your book of records to the same page, paragraph, line, and word where the initial wounding is recorded. All your partner has to do is consistently behave toward you with empathy, respect, and authenticity— and healing happens. Unfortunately, if your partner hasn't learned how to overcome their defensive behaviors so that they can meet your needs, you will be wounded even more deeply.

This is the potential in intimate relating. The possibility for being healed depends upon your partner's willingness to meet your needs in the very ways that are the most difficult for them. They will have to stretch into reclaiming the parts of themselves that they previously discontinued because of fear. Of course the same scenario is playing with you.

The potential for mutual healing lies in your and your partner's commitment to mutual stretching. You will both win, or you will both lose. You are learning how to create your dream relationship, and whether or not you realize it, your dream is now a conscious choice. All that is necessary is for you both to stretch into giving what the other needs and stretch into receiving what you need. Remember, don't jump ship when the waters get rough, for no attempt that you make in life will require more courage, perseverance, and willingness to risk as entering the new ERA of knowing and being known by another. And no other endeavor is more potentially rewarding.

The ERA Process is an ideal tool for learning to stretch, and as your relationship transforms, you and your partner will simultaneously experience personal growth and healing. So in addition to having a deep and lasting love relationship, each of you can reach a level of maturity and wholeness in which you are living life as a delightfully spontaneous adventure.

Make It Known

1. As you and your partner consciously and intentionally apply what you're learning, your relationship transforms.
2. Unless both partners are doing the work of intimacy building, after a time, continuing to try will result in a self-sacrificial and abusive partnership. This dynamic is lose/lose.
3. Perhaps the only wholesome reason for dissolving an intimate love relationship is that you or your partner is not willing to do the work.
4. The process that occurs as you begin to communicate with one another in a healing and growth-producing manner is called the Transformation Stage, and is the fourth stage of intimate relating.
5. The interpersonal skills that are necessary in a mutually beneficial and intimate relationship are empathy, respect, and authenticity (ERA).
   Empathy: Understanding an Other's thoughts and feelings from their perspective.
   Respect: Concern, regard, and appreciation for the Other's experiences, feelings, and potential.
   Authenticity: Expressing One's truth in an appropriate and constructive manner.
6. The basic skill on which the other two rest is *empathy*. The way to accomplish empathy is to focus on the Other and pay attention with an open heart.
7. What is sent influences your ability to stay open and pay attention so that you can "get it."
8. You cannot get away from the fact that as a human being, you have a history that operates at an unconscious level to

influence your present life experiences. Evolving beyond the limitations imposed by your history requires the cooperation of both partners.

9. The more precisely you match the words, tone, energy, expressions, inflections, and gestures of your partner— the more they will feel understood. And being understood is a basic human need. (Being able *to* understand is also a basic human need, and when you are empathic, you derive this side benefit.)

10. Empathy alone is not enough for a healing growth encounter. The other two interpersonal skills, *respect* and *authenticity*, must also be in place in order for empathy to be wholesome.

11. Agreement isn't necessary to validate another when a respectful attitude is in place.

12. Without empathy and respect, authenticity is impossible. "The truth, the whole truth, and nothing but the truth" is *not* the definition of authenticity.

13. When you put words to your defenses, the things you say because you're scared and alienated, it comes out as criticism, judgment, or manipulation. This is adaptive behavior and therefore inauthentic. Authenticity is the communication of your reality *underneath* the fear.

14. Learning that you cannot speak for another, not just because it's thoughtless or rude, but because you truly cannot *know* another's truth, is an awareness that comes with maturing.

15. The vulnerability necessary for intimacy building comes from both being open to hear your partner's reality so that you can know him/her, and saying your authentic truth so that your partner can know you.

16. All three interpersonal skills are incorporated into a transforming procedure known as "The ERA Process,"

which is a highly structured communicative process that promotes intimacy as well as personal growth and development.

17. Conflict in an intimate relationship is more than a failure to communicate, it is the result of both partners' unresolved developmental issues.

18. Both the Sender and the Receiver have responsibilities in their roles within the The ERA Process.

19. How you send (tone of voice, inflections, body language, eye contact, etc.) and the content of your send are factors that influence the Receiver. Three indicators that the Sender is not fulfilling his/her responsibility in creating a wholesome interaction are: the Sender is 1) being critical, 2) attempting to manipulate an outcome, and/or 3) making assumptions that s/he *knows* the Receiver.

20. How you receive, and the content of your mirroring, influence the Sender. Indicators that the Receiver is not creating a wholesome interaction are: the Receiver is 1) demonstrating self-absorbed *Reactivity*, 2) reflecting inaccurately, 3) being inattentive, 4) thinking, 5) analyzing, 6) interpreting, 7) being distracted, 8) interrupting, and/or 9) becoming bored.

21. The experience of equal reciprocity is essential in The ERA Process.

22. An *Intimate Partner Profile* Match partner is the perfect person to heal you, because the unconscious part of you has already accepted her/him as the early caregiver from whom your major wounds came. Your unconscious opens your book of records to the same page, paragraph, and line where the initial wounding is recorded. All your partner has to do is consistently behave toward you with

empathy, respect, and authenticity, and healing happens. Unfortunately, if your partner hasn't learned how to overcome their defensive behaviors so that s/he can meet your needs, you are wounded even more deeply. And vice versa.

23. The potential for mutual healing lies in your commitment to mutual stretching (growing). Both you and your partner will win, or you will both lose. All that is needed is for you to move into *The New ERA of Intimacy*. Remember, hang in there when it doesn't go smoothly, for no attempt that we make in life will require more courage, perseverance, and willingness to risk as knowing and being known by another. And no other endeavor is more potentially rewarding.

Make It Personal

As an initiation into learning to enter *The New ERA of Intimacy,* engage in the eleven steps of The ERA Process as both Sender and Receiver, with your partner if you are presently in a primary relationship; otherwise, with someone willing to practice with you, for at least 20 minutes, twice a week, for a minimum of six weeks. Make sure each person spends an equal amount of time in each role.

Stage Five: Real Love 8

I'm as beautiful as you are

You were born together, and together you shall
    be forevermore.
You shall be together when the white wings of
    death scatter your days.
Aye, you shall be together even in the silent
    memory of God.
But let there be spaces in your togetherness,
And let the winds of the heavens dance between
    you.

Love one another, but make not a bond of love:
Let it rather be a moving sea between the shores
    of your souls.
Fill each other's cup but drink not from one cup.
Give one another of your bread but eat not from

the same loaf.

Sing and dance together and be joyous, but let
    each one of you be alone,

Even as the strings of a lute are alone though they
    quiver with the same music.

Give your hearts, but not into each other's keeping.

For only the hand of Life can contain your hearts.

And stand together yet not too near together:

For the pillars of the temple stand apart,

And the oak tree and the cypress grow not in each
    other's shadow.

                —Kahlil Gibran, *The Prophet* (1923)

---

*Y*OU ARE LEARNING THAT YOU DON'T HAVE THE OPTION of choosing between a healthy love relationship and your own growth and personal fulfillment. You were designed to have it *all*! Our work together has shown that the path you must travel to claim your dream relationship is the *identical* path that will enable you to develop into a healthy and fulfilled individual.

Remember, you can only love another to the degree that you can love yourself. *You and I must be committed to having our own needs met as well as to meeting the needs of the other.* We must do both—in order to do either. Our old either/or way of thinking makes it difficult for us to get our arms around this truth. In all the places where we reach an impasse with another, we suffer from the illusion that if we meet the needs of our partner, our own needs will go unmet, or conversely, if our partner meets our needs, theirs will go unmet. I trust that I've challenged you to let go of these either/or illusions, and that your grip is loosening. For indeed, "I am as beautiful as you are."

Perhaps it is time to say that experiencing Real Love does not mean feeling happy all the time. That would not be living, not paying attention to what's going on, not being real. Just as "love" in mature love is not primarily about feelings, it is about intentional behavior, so "happily" in happily-ever-after is also not primarily about feelings. "Happily" is about being fully alive, which means noticing all of your *feelings*, experiencing all of your *senses*, exploiting all of your *thinking* capacity, and utilizing all of your *kinesthetic* potential. (Notice that feelings, although abundantly present, represents only *one* of these four important human functions.)

Love, in *The New ERA of Intimacy* means "I am willing to do what you need of me, which you enable me to do, by doing what I need of you." Incidentally, if you're wondering if good feelings are present in this era of mature love, *nothing feels better* than this. And if this definition of love doesn't read as smoothly as you would like, others far wiser than I have said it far better:

"What you do not want done to yourself, do not do to others."

—Confucius (551-479 BC)
The Chinese Classics, Vol. I:
The Confucian Analects

". . . all things whatsoever ye would that men should do to you, do ye even so to them."

—Jesus (The *Bible*, Matthew 7:12)

Referred to as "The Golden Rule" and quoted more commonly as "Do unto others as you would have them do unto you," this prescription for living has been recommended by those most widely revered and followed throughout history. But the "rule" as commonly quoted is easily misunderstood. A more personal understanding of the meaning of this grand rule is: "Do unto others as *they would have you do* unto them."

You are wise to want both a satisfying love relationship *and* a fulfilling personal life. By growing up and becoming a psychological adult, you can have both. But growing up, maturing, doesn't happen in the "Aha!" of an insight. It is an organic progression, and eventually, the healing and growth-producing experiences will accumulate until a mature critical mass of wholesomeness is formed. In the meantime, what so many have gone about preaching, we can gently go about practicing.

Think back to the image of your true essence—compacted pulsating energy. You pulse out (give or *send* to another) and you pulse in (take in or *receive* from another). And this pulse must be in balance, otherwise you are in pain and travail, and you feel less and less alive. Your out-of-balance influence on those around you will be painful to them, and they will feel less and less alive as well. *Your life and the lives of others literally hang in the balance, and the fate of one is the fate of all.*

Embracing this understanding requires that you alter the very way that you think. The archaic beliefs that have kept you stuck in unhappiness and loneliness cannot survive the quantum leap in consciousness that will result from your regularly engaging in The ERA Process. Within your committed primary love relationship as well as with other fellow human beings, as you internalize the spirit and discipline of the process, you will create a world in which learning and growing are no longer hard work.

The focus moves beyond solving relationship problems, into the delight of using your talents to make the world a better place. Being alive is exciting and exhilarating! Spontaneous interacting is the order of the day. Life is a celebration. This is Stage Five—*Real Love.*

". . . I could have missed the pain, but I'd have had to miss the dance."

—*The Dance*, lyrics by Tony Arata,
recorded by Garth Brooks

From now on, it's up to you (and up to your partner when you enter a committed relationship)! You have the information and you have the process. All that's remaining is that you learn to dance to the rhythm of your Being. The more you practice, the more skillful you become. The steps are simple, but learning to execute them is challenging.

Dancing with another is complex. Staying in step with one another requires that you both pay close attention. Missteps can be painful. A minor miscalculation of stepping too close and crowding, or conversely, of stepping too distant and disconnecting, can throw you and your partner off-balance. Balance and harmony is regained most quickly when one partner compensates for the other's mistakes. When done artfully, the mistake disappears.

You may be wise to engage a teacher who can coach you in learning the structured steps. A skillful teacher observes the patterns that lead to your abandoning the structure and helps you "nip them in the bud." S/he also helps you learn ways to stay balanced within yourself while staying with your partner. Then s/he guides you to consistently practice the precise corrective adjustments, so that you and your partner each carry your own weight, balanced at all times, while simultaneously responding to the smallest nuance of the other's movements. "Light as a feather," is how we experience a dance partner who is perfectly grounded and balanced.

In dancing, balance means that all our weight is firmly supported by one foot *or* the other at all times; *balanced* with weight equally distributed on both feet is an illusion in dancing. Some would say this is a good news/bad news phenomenon. The good news is that we are immediately available to take the next step and we are clear as to which foot will take that step (it is, of course, the foot that is not supporting your weight—literally, the only foot you *can* move). The bad news is that being balanced on one foot makes you vulnerable. You can be knocked off-balance very easily. You cannot dance masterfully unless you are totally vulnerable to and interdependent with your partner.

A good partner not only respects your balance while balancing their own weight, they are also in prominent and comfortable contact, available to step forward, backward, sideways, in small or sweeping steps, in rhythm with the music of the moment. They show up, providing at times a forceful boundary that stops you, and at other times, a flowing presence that moves with you. Both partners must be listening to the same music; attentive; disciplined; physically, mentally, and psychologically fit; and committed to the sport of couple dancing. You dance best with those who are at your level of expertise and with whom you practice.

In dancing, both look good, or both look bad—win/win or lose/lose. When one of you is out of step, the other is automatically out of step also. Even when you cover for one another, you both experience the momentary jolt of "off the beat." However, as you bypass the inclination to criticize and blame, and focus on getting back on beat, you will both grow. Gradually you will each claim your potential to establish and maintain your own inner balance, while being available and vulnerable to your partner.

Whether or not "practice makes perfect," there is no doubt that persistence will pay off as you and your partner develop toward maturity. And one day you will find that together, you are dancing spontaneously, creatively and joyfully, *Making Real Love Happen!*

Perhaps the best payoff of all—in the long term—is that in *The New ERA of Intimacy*, you will build better nests for your children who will build even better nests for their children . . . and so on and so on. . . .

Glossary

adaptive behavior—the programmed behavior that is automatically exhibited when you are reactive.

authenticity—expressing one's truth in an appropriate and constructive manner; one of the three major rapport-building interpersonal (relationship) skills.

awareness stage—the potential third stage of a primary intimate relationship. Entering this stage requires intention and work—working to understand oneself and one's partner better and to understand the dynamics and skills of intimate relating more fully.

behavior change request—requesting that another change a behavior; the request is stated in specific, positive, and behavioral terms.

compacted pulsating energy—the essence of a living being.

criticism—anything you say, do, think, or feel while focusing on fault. It can manifest as a thought, a look, a gesture, a posturing of the body, a verbal tone, an act, or an utterance. Every criticism is projection and is never beneficial.

discern—to mentally discriminate; to recognize as separate and different.

empathy—understanding an other's thoughts and feelings from their perspective; the most basic of the three major rapport-building interpersonal (relationship) skills.

engram—the trace or impression left in cells subjected to a frequently repeated stimulus.

ERA—an acronym for empathy, respect, and authenticity.

The ERA Process—a highly structured communicative process that promotes intimacy as well as personal growth and development.

falling in love—perceiving enough traits and characteristics in another that are similar to those encoded in your intimate partner profile to trigger an intimate partner profile match. This match releases exhilarating feelings stored long ago. This is a regressive experience that utilizes projection.

falling out of love—the disappointing experience of having the exhilarating feelings (those that were evidence of being in love) disappear. This occurs when the partner is no longer perceived as an intimate partner profile match.

healing—receiving what you've historically needed (but not previously gotten) in just the way you need it, for as often as it takes for a wound to diminish. It results in the dissolving of self-hatred.

Intimate Partner Profile (IPP)—the composite of all of the impacting images of and experiences with your early caregivers, along with your responses to those experiences, that are encoded in your memory banks.

Intimate Partner Profile Match (IPPM)—a person who

matches your intimate partner profile closely enough that s/he activates a replay of some of the images/feelings stored in your IPP.

key to your heart—what you need to feel loved; i.e., having the desires behind your unmet childhood needs, met.

maturing—an organic progression within human beings in which healing and growth-producing experiences accumulate until a critical mass of wholesomeness is formed.

maximizing—one of the two forms of reactivity; the body's expanding process in response to the perception that another is unavailable or unresponsive, leaving you feeling neglected or abandoned—unseen, unheard, not valued, not noticed.

minimizing—one of the two forms of reactivity; the body's constricting process in response to the perception that another is attempting to control or manipulate you, leaving you feeling intruded upon—smothered, not free to be yourself.

mirror/mirroring—used as a verb: the receiver saying back exactly what the sender has said—using the same words with the same tone, pace, and inflection—and manifesting the same nonverbal behaviors (as close to a video recording as possible) as the sender expresses.

pain—the uncomfortable feeling experienced when your natural pulsation is interfered with; the hurting feeling that accompanies perceived threat.

power struggle stage—the second stage of a primary intimate relationship; characterized by both partners attempting to force the other to meet their needs in certain anticipated ways.

primary caregiver—a person responsible for your care when you were young; your parents and/or whoever served as a surrogate parent.

primary reactive style—the reactive style that you experienced most often and most intensely when you were a child. It will become the reactive style that you generalize when you can't clearly distinguish the nature of a threat.

projection—the process of perceiving in another what is really in yourself.

reactivity—the automatic, internal response your body manifests whenever you perceive threat.

real love—the consistent and joyful willingness between two people to give what the other needs in exactly the way they need it.

real love stage—the potential fifth stage in a primary intimate relationship. This stage is reached when partners consistently demonstrate real love toward one another: "I am willing to do what you need of me, which you enable me to do, by doing what I need of you."

receiver—the person who is receiving communication.

receiving—the act of receiving communication; i.e., listening, observing, paying attention to the sender.

respect—concern, regard, and appreciation for the other's experiences, feelings, and potential; one of the three major rapport-building interpersonal (relationship) skills.

romantic love stage—the first stage of a primary intimate relationship. This stage is activated by an intimate partner profile match. The more intense your feelings, the more likely you are engaging in regression and projection. This stage always comes to an end, but it is an opportunity to glimpse what is possible to create in the future as a reality.

self-hatred—to identify yourself as responsible for your pain and disadvantaged state and conclude that you are unworthy of having your needs or wants met.

sender—the person who is communicating.

sending—the act of communicating; includes many forms: talking, gesturing, facial expressions, body language, etc.

stretching—behaving in intentional ways that reclaim the discontinued behaviors that were too dangerous to maintain at an earlier time. Stretching, when practiced consistently, leads to personal growth as well as healing for the one being gifted.

transformation stage—the potential fourth stage of a primary intimate relationship. This period is entered as partners consciously and intentionally practice what they have learned in the awareness stage.

validation—a communication that what the sender has communicated to the receiver makes sense, is important, valuable, and fully respected.

wound—pain recorded in your body.

Bibliography

Barks, Coleman. *Rumi: The Book of Love: Poems of Ecstasy and Longing.* Harper San Francisco, 2003.

Beveridge, Martha. *Loving Your Partner without Losing Your Self.* Hunter House Publishers, 2001.

Bly, Robert. *Times Alone: Selected Poems of Antonio Machado.* Wesleyan University Press, 1983.

Bonney, Merl E. *The Normal Personality.* McCutchan Publishing Corporation, Berkeley, California, 1969.

Bowlby, John. *Attachment and Loss*, Volume I: Attachment. Basic Books, New York, 1983.

Bowlby, John. *Attachment and Loss*, Volume II: Separation. Basic Books, New York, 1986.

Bowlby, John. *Attachment and Loss*, Volume III: Loss. Basic Books, New York, 1986.

De Castillejo, Irene Claremont. *Knowing Woman: A Feminine Psychology*. Boston: Shambhala Publications, Inc., 1990.

De Lubac, Henri. *The Eternal Feminine: A Study on the Poem by Teilhard de Chardin, followed by Teilhard and the Problems of Today*. New York: Collins, 1968.

Dickinson, Saundra. *Love That Works: The 12 Foundation Stones*. Maryland: Recovery Communications, Inc., 2002, 2003.

Einstein, Albert. "The Goal of Human Existence," *Out of My Later Years*. New York: Carol Publishing Group, 1995.

Ekman, P. "Cross-Cultural Studies of Facial Expression," *Darwin and Facial Expression: A Century of Research in Review*. New York: Academic Press, 1973.

Fifer, W. P., and C. M. Moon. "The role of mother's voice in the organization of brain function in the newborn." *Acta Paediatrica Supplement*, 397:86-93, 1994.

Fisher, Helen. *Why We Love—The Nature and Chemistry of Romantic Love*. New York: Henry Holt and Company, 2004.

Freud, Sigmund. *The Standard Edition of the Complete Psychological Works of Sigmund Freud*, J. Strachey (ed.). London: Hogarth Press, 1953.

Gibran, Kahlil. *The Prophet*. New York: Alfred A Knopf, 1923, Twenty-ninth Printing, July 1988.

Hendrix, Harville. *Getting the Love You Want, A Guide for Couples*, New York: Henry Holt & Company, 1988.

Hill, Clara E, and Karen M. O'Brien, *Helping Skills: Facilitating Exploration, Insight, and Action*, Washington, D.C.: American Psychological Association, 1999.

Hofer, M.A. "Early relationships as regulators of infant physiology and behavior." *Acta Paediatrica Supplement*, 387:9-18, 1994.

Insel, T. R. "Oxytocin: a neuropeptide for affiliation: evidence from behavioral, receptor, autoradiographic, and comparative studies." *Psychoneuroendocrinology*, 17 (I): 3-35, 1992.

Karen, R. *Becoming Attached: First Relationships and How They Shape Our Capacity to Love*. New York: Oxford University Press, 1994.

Kavanaugh, James. *There Are Men Too Gentle To Live Among Wolves*. New York: E. P. Dutton & Co., Inc., 1970.

Kihlstrom, J., T. Barnhardt, and D. Tataryn. "The psychological unconscious: found, lost, and regained." *American Psychologist*, 47 (6):788-91, 1992.

Kraemer, G. W. "A psychobiological theory of attachment." *Behavioral and Brain Sciences*, 15: 493-541,1992.

Lewis, Jerry. *Marriage as a Search for Healing*. New York: Brunner/Mazel, Inc., Publishers, 1997.

Lewis, Thomas, Fari Amini, and Richard Lannon. *A General Theory of Love*. New York: Random House, 2000.

Love, Patricia. *The Truth About Love: The Highs, the Lows, and How You Can Make It Last Forever*. New York: Fireside, 2001.

Mahler, Margaret. *On Human Symbiosis and the Vicissitudes of Individuation: Infantile Psychosis*. New York: International Universities Press, 1968.

May, Rollo. *Love and Will*. New York: W. W. Norton and Company, Inc., 1969.

MacLean, Paul. *A Triune Concept of the Brain and Behavior*, Toronto: University of Toronto Press, 1973.

MacLean, Paul. *The Triune Brain in Evolution*. New York: Plenum Press, 1990.

McKuen, Rod. *Stanyan Street & Other Sorrows*. New York: Random House, 1954, Ninth Printing 1966.

Ornish, Dean. *Love and Survival: The Scientific Basis for the Healing Power of Intimacy*. New York: Harper Collins, 1998.

Penfield, Wilder. *The Mystery of Mind: A Critical Study of Consciousness and the Human Brain*. Princeton: Princeton University Press, 1975.

Pines, Ayala Malach. *Falling In Love, Why We Choose The Lovers We Choose*. New York: Routledge, 1999.

Prather, Hugh. *Notes to Myself*, Utah: Real People Press, 1970.

Sagan, Carl. *Billions & Billions, Thoughts on Life and Death at the Brink of the Millennium*. New York: Ballantine Books, 1997.

Siegel, Daniel J. *The Developing Mind: Toward a Neurobiology of Interpersonal Experience*. New York: The Guilford Press, 1999.

Siegel, Daniel J. *Parenting from the Inside Out*. New York: Jeremy P. Tarcher/Putman, 2003.

Stuart, Richard. *Helping Couples Change: A Social Learning Approach to Marital Therapy*. New York: The Guilford Press, 1980.

Truax, Charles B., and Robert R. Carkhuff. *Toward Effective Counseling and Psychotherapy: Training and Practice*. Chicago: Aldine Publishing Company, 1967.

Wyse, Lois. *A Weeping Eye Can Never See.* New York: Doubleday & Company, Inc., 1972.

Zohar, Danah. *The Quantum Self, Human Nature and Consciousness defined by the New Physics.* New York: Quill/ William Morrow, 1990.

Index

About the Author

Joyce Buckner, Ph.D., is internationally recognized as a leading authority on relationships, intimacy, and the dialogical process.

A licensed psychologist and marriage and family therapist in private practice for more than 30 years, Dr. Buckner has worked extensively with hundreds of couples in intimate relationships and individuals struggling with relationship issues. Having made seminal contributions to the theory and practice of Imago Relationship Therapy, she has now developed her own model—The New ERA of Intimacy. In the last 20 years, Dr. Buckner has trained mental health providers from around the globe in relationship therapy. She appears as a relationship expert on international radio and television talk shows, including *The Oprah Winfrey Show.*

Dr. Buckner is also a former professor and academic department head at the University of Texas at Arlington. She is certified by the Council for the National Registry of Health Service Providers in Psychology, is past president of the international

Association for Imago Relationship Therapy, and is listed in *Who's Who of the World*. She and her husband, Sanford Reitman, M.D., have six adult children and eight grandchildren and live on a ranch west of Fort Worth, Texas. Dr. Buckner can be reached at joyce@joycebuckner.com.